Discover *your*
Psychic Type

About the Author

Sherrie Dillard has been a professional psychic and medium for over twenty years. She uses her psychic abilities to help clients around the world, and she has worked with police departments in several states to uncover information in murder and missing-person investigations.

Dillard has taught classes and workshops on intuition, spiritual development, and spiritual healing both nationally and internationally. She teaches a course on intuition development at Duke Continuing Studies, Duke University.

Please visit her website at www.sherriedillard.com.

To Write to the Author

If you wish to contact the author or would like more information about this book, please write to the author in care of Llewellyn Worldwide and we will forward your request. Both the author and publisher appreciate hearing from you and learning of your enjoyment of this book and how it has helped you. Llewellyn Worldwide cannot guarantee that every letter written to the author can be answered, but all will be forwarded. Please write to:

Sherrie Dillard
⁒ Llewellyn Worldwide
2143 Wooddale Drive, Dept. 978-0-7387-1278-9
Woodbury, MN 55125-2989, U.S.A.

Please enclose a self-addressed stamped envelope for reply,
or $1.00 to cover costs. If outside the USA, enclose
an international postal reply coupon.

Many of Llewellyn's authors have websites with additional information and resources. For more information, please visit our website at http://www.llewellyn.com

Discover *your* Psychic Type

Developing and Using Your Natural Intuition

SHERRIE DILLARD

Llewellyn Publications
Woodbury, Minnesota

First Edition
Fourth Printing, 2009

Book design by Steffani Sawyer
Cover image of leaf, water, trees, sky © 2008 Comstock
Cover image of fire © 2008 PhotoDisc
Cover design by Ellen Dahl
Editing by Brett Fechheimer
Llewellyn is a registered trademark of Llewellyn Worldwide, Ltd.

Dillard, Sherrie, 1958–
Discover your psychic type : developing and using your natural intuition / Sherrie Dillard. — 1st ed.
    p. cm.
Includes bibliographical references.
ISBN 978-0-7387-1278-9
1. Psychic ability. 2. Intuition. I. Title.
BF1040.D55 2008
133.8—dc22

2007046515

Llewellyn Worldwide does not participate in, endorse, or have any authority or responsibility concerning private business transactions between our authors and the public.

All mail addressed to the author is forwarded but the publisher cannot, unless specifically instructed by the author, give out an address or phone number.

Any Internet references contained in this work are current at publication time, but the publisher cannot guarantee that a specific location will continue to be maintained. Please refer to the publisher's website for links to authors' websites and other sources.

Llewellyn Publications
A Division of Llewellyn Worldwide, Ltd.
2143 Wooddale Drive, Dept. 978-0-7387-1278-9
Woodbury, Minnesota 55125-2989, U.S.A.
www.llewellyn.com

Printed in the United States of America

To my husband, Kenni, and my children, Aiden and Mariah,
for all of their patience, love, and support.

Contents

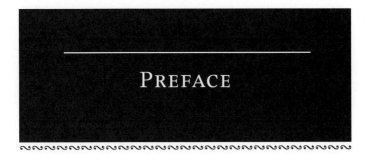

Once again it is time for the annual family reunion. For generations, every summer, the family that now spreads out over twelve states meets in a different location to visit, celebrate, and catch up everyone's news. For the past several years the family has asked Scott to choose the date and location for the reunion. He seems to have a special knack for finding the right place and time to get together. Ever since he took over this responsibility, plans have run smoothly.

Scott loves numbers. He is a computer software developer and part-time numerology enthusiast. He pays attention to the patterns and coincidences of certain numbers that emerge throughout his personal and work-related affairs. His interest in numerology began when he started noticing the number four appearing in clusters of three throughout his day, including in phone numbers, on the speedometer of his car, and in confirmation and registration numbers. He often wakes in the early morning to see the same sequence 4:44 on his digital clock. When he sees this series of numbers, he feels confident that he is being guided and that he's on the right track.

When Scott makes plans for the family reunion, he looks for this sequence of fours. He looks at the dates for the event, its location on the map, the addresses of possible hotels and parks, and then he looks for the number four. When the number four emerges in his search for the perfect date and location for the family reunion, Scott takes note. When a sequence of three fours emerges, he closes his eyes and visualizes the location. If his perception of this image has the right energy and brightness, then he feels confident in making plans.

Scott knows that the number four represents practicality. *"This is perfect,"* he thinks, *"I am a practical man."*

Liza folds her shirts and pants and places them neatly in her suitcase. She has not been to a family reunion for a few years, and she is looking forward to seeing her brother's new baby girl and visiting with the other more distant relatives that she knows will be attending this year. She will miss the family matriarch, her grandmother Eleanor who died last fall. Grandmother Eleanor had kept the peace in the family for years. There had been an ongoing rift in the family caused by a long-standing financial misunderstanding between her two aunts. Now with Grandmother Eleanor no longer alive, Liza wonders if the precarious peace between the two women will be broken during the reunion.

Liza, thinking of her aunts and the potential tension between the two of them, closes her eyes and imagines them facing one another. She feels the conflict and stress between them as she takes a deep breath and focuses on her love for both of them. Liza imagines sending this love to her aunts, and she continues to feel warmth, affection, and peace surrounding them. Liza has found that when she feels anxious about her children or her husband, this loving meditation soothes her nerves and helps to ease the burdens or stresses that her family may be feeling. She thinks to herself that each day leading up to the reunion she will take a few minutes and send love and harmony to her aunts.

Bill rises at dawn every morning. He likes to start work early while the day is still cool. After a short drive through a thick grove of cedar and pine trees, he enters the park gates and surveys the grounds. The good weather has brought more people than normal this year to the park. Soon he knows that the laughter of children playing in the clear river and green fields and the smell of grilled hamburgers will overtake the quiet peacefulness of the morning. Bill imagines his ancestors, proud Cherokees who once lived on this land, enjoying the happiness that still permeates the hills. Bill chose to work at the park for this reason. He feels closer to his people and to his heritage just knowing that their spirits still reside here, undisturbed by the bulldozers and construction that has overtaken much of the surrounding area.

Bill walks slowly to the river and notices a hawk perched on a tree close to the water's edge. Bill then faces the four directions one by one—north, south, east, and west—and as he does this, he asks for the blessing of the Great Spirit. He takes a moment to thank the Great Spirit for the contentment that he has found in his life. He then heads toward the groundskeeping shed to take out the lawn mower and clippers, passing under the large picnic pavilion on his way. He remembers that there is a large family reunion that will soon fill the empty space. He thinks of his own family—the babies, the young people making their way into the world, and the elders proud of the accomplishments and the timeless love they share. He feels the connection of family and love.

Bill reaches into his pocket and feels his well-worn leather pouch filled with cedar and tobacco leaves. He carries this with him wherever he goes, always aware that an opportunity for a prayer and request for blessings from the Great Spirit might present itself. It now feels like such a time, so again he faces the four directions—the north, south, east, and west. He chants a prayer and offers tobacco to the ancestors and the spirits of the hills, requesting blessings of peace, harmony, and love for the family that will soon fill this pavilion.

Katie feels the cool water on her toes. She sees in the water's reflection the sun and clouds, and she imagines herself high in the sky floating above the trees and the people. Her cousins call to her to join them in a game of hide-and-go-seek. She runs to hide. She is only six and not very big, so she knows that it will be easy for her to crawl under some bushes and be well-hidden. But before she can hide, she hears her mother's voice announcing that it's time to eat.

Katie is excited; her grandpa, cousins, aunts, and uncles are all here, some of whom she barely remembers from a year ago. She has seen the watermelon, cakes, and hotdogs on top of the colorful tablecloths, and she can't wait to eat. But instead of eating, the family first makes a circle and joins hands. They say that it's time to say a prayer in thankfulness for each other and the abundance in their lives. Tears come to some of the grownups' eyes as they say a special prayer for Great-Grandma Eleanor, who died last fall. But Katie doesn't cry. She sees Great-Grandma Eleanor standing close to Grandpa. She is pretty, she has light all around her, and she is smiling. Katie gives a little wave to Great-Grandma Eleanor, who winks back at her.

Is Scott having a run of good luck in choosing the location and date for the family reunion each year? Is it a coincidence that there seems to be less arguing and conflict since he has taken on this responsibility? Is his interest in numbers just a quirky hobby? Can Scott access unknown or hidden information in numbers and patterns of numbers?

Is Liza able to feel what her aunts feel from hundreds of miles away? Is her concern for an emotionally stressful interaction between her aunts at the family reunion just her own pessimism?

Is it possible that Liza can send love and harmony to her aunts, and in so doing affect their feelings and attitudes?

Is Bill really able to sense his ancestors in the hills where they once lived? Or is he simply a nice man who thinks of others? Can his offerings of tobacco to the Great Spirit really bring blessings to a family he has never met?

Does young Katie have a very active imagination, or can she really see and make contact with her deceased great-grandmother? Is it possible that in years to come she will continue to make contact with those who have passed over?

What might appear to be random coincidence may instead be the carefully orchestrated coming together of meaningful events and influences. Many of these influences emanate from the nonphysical spheres, which I refer to as *spirit*. The spiritual and physical realms continuously respond to and affect one another.

We intersect with others and help one another in a multitude of ways, even when we are completely unaware that we are doing so. There is an intelligent and loving energy—which I refer to as *Spirit*, *God*, and *Divine Spirit*—that we can trust and with which we can work in unison.

We may be guided to know this energy through our intuition. As we become more aware of how intuition naturally flows through us, we will be better able to use and expand this inherent gift that we all possess. Our intuition may be as individualized as we are. All intuition is not alike.

Scott, for example, may be a mental intuitive, someone who receives guidance and information through thought and contemplation. Mental intuitives are especially adept at seeing patterns, systems, and methods. Liza could be an emotional intuitive, an individual who is empathetic and receives information through emotional energy. An emotional intuitive can reach out and perceive feelings in others, even those whom they have never met. Bill is possibly a physical intuitive. Physical intuitives are attuned to and able to read physical energy. They are connected to the natural world and have a deep love for the earth and her creatures. Katie may be a spiritual intuitive. She is able to see and connect with loved ones who have passed over. Her intuition may surface through dreams, visions, and spiritual seeing.

Which type of intuitive are you? The following pages will help you to find out.

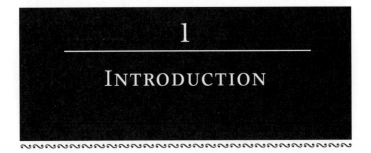

1

INTRODUCTION

Our natural curiosity pushes us to lift the curtain of consciousness. The unknown inspires us. We are compelled to discover what lies beyond our everyday experiences, thoughts, and emotions. Over the years, people from all walks of life have come to my office to visit with the unseen. People from all income levels, occupations, races, and religious beliefs have come, seeking wisdom and contact with the spiritual world.

Working with such people, I have learned that we have an innate understanding of the unseen realms. Even though we generally deny this aspect of our intelligence, we are still able to connect and interact with what is of spirit.

Within us lies the core truth of all that is. It is through knowing ourselves that we come to know all of life. In this knowing we are led to the experience of unconditional love, beauty, and wisdom. We are led into the experience of divinity, which we may call God, Universal Life Force, Divine Intelligence, or the Supreme Being. Many of us have had encounters with spiritual guides, angels, or other holy beings that break through our normal sense of what is possible and bring us closer to the universal all-knowing. They are our friends, our loved ones, and they know us better than anyone else. As we uncover our ability to communicate with Spirit, we reveal the depth of our own divine nature.

Intuitive versus Psychic

Intuition is our guide into this vast sea of unconditional love and intelligence. *Intuition* is defined as the ability to understand or know something immediately and without conscious reasoning. Intuition is an instinctive knowing, an impression.[1] We have all had moments, many of them, when we knew the truth.

It seems to be not so much a matter of whether or not we are intuitive, but where and how our intuition comes forth in our lives. Intuition usually surfaces in the areas of our personalities with which we are most comfortable. It may emerge, for example, through our feelings and emotions. For some it surfaces in the physical body as an ache, a pain, a lightness, or other bodily awareness. Others among us may use our intuition most often through our thoughts, our processing of concepts and ideas. Or we might feel most in touch with our intuition through our spiritual and religious pursuits, in prayer and in meditation.

We tend to think of intuition as coming through for us in breakthrough *aha!* moments, but most of the time, intuition is quiet and still. It does not rattle us. It is more like a gentle nudge or a persistent feeling or thought. In fact, our intuition is often so much a part of our lives that it feels natural and normal, and many people do not feel that they are intuitive because to them intuition does not feel unusual. We can become so accustomed to using our intuition that we call it *common sense* or *the obvious*.

Al is a successful businessman. He was formerly the CEO of a thriving vitamin company, and he now works as a business consultant. Al was asked by a company to investigate the possibility of acquiring some smaller, similar companies. He visited the companies in question. He also sought out a few other small businesses he thought were interesting, and along the way he met a young man who had started a small but innovative company. Although this young man, just twenty-four years old, did not have much experience, Al told me that when they met he felt an immediate connection with him. This young man, Al said, did not have the kind of qualifications that the company required, but Al was still excited and felt determined to work with this young man and his new ideas. Eventually, Al convinced the company for which he was consulting to buy the young man's concept, and a lucrative affiliation was established. Despite the fact that the young man did not have all the requirements that the company was looking for, Al somehow "knew" that their connection would be successful. Al told me he feels that he has "good instincts." I would argue that this is an example of intuition.

For some people, intuition is a curiosity, an afterthought, or an interesting concept. It can seem irrational and illogical. We have an antiquated belief system surrounding this common and frequently used function. Perhaps this is to some extent because being intuitive and being psychic are so closely related. To be intuitive is to be able *to know without knowing how you know*. To be psychic seems to be a step up from that, to have *the ability to access at will extrasensory information and knowledge*. Being psychic is simply a more refined and developed form of intuition. Most people have preconceived ideas of what being psychic means. When people hear the word *psychic*, all kinds of images usually surface in their minds: a television infomercial, a neon sign promising to change our luck from bad to good, strange and outlandish phenomena, and perhaps someone who claims to have special powers and requires large sums of money to help us out of impending doom.

There are some people who wonder why those who claim to be psychic don't know what will happen in their own day-to-day lives. I have heard such people remark that psychics should know when they will get sick, get laid off, have an accident, or should know the answers to game show questions. Psychics, many reason, should know everything that will occur in the future.

Yet we don't expect that much accuracy from most of science and medicine. Doctors know a lot about many illnesses.

They know what tumors look like and how cancer grows in our bodies and cells. They know roughly how long someone may live once diagnosed with cancer. They even know what other organs certain cancers may spread to. Still, many, many people die every year from cancer. Doctors can't cure many types of cancer. Many chronic illnesses such as diabetes and AIDS are incurable. However, all that doesn't stop us from going to doctors when we're ill. We listen to them and believe what they tell us. In most cases, we trust our lives to modern medicine.

We were once absolutely positive that there were no other planets in our solar system. Later, our telescopes revealed to us a certain number of planets, and we believed that this finite number of planets in our solar system must forever be a scientific fact. But a short time ago, a professor who had just lectured on this topic unexpectedly discovered another small planet within our solar system that we had no idea existed.

Advanced intelligence gathering is in place as part of the American defense system. The government and military gather intelligence through highly sophisticated equipment each and every day, yet the tragedy of 9/11 still happened. We didn't know about all the plots against us, and we were not aware that our lives were in such danger.

Billions of dollars are spent every year on medicine, science, technology, and defense. We teach, we train, we educate ourselves. Still, we are made aware each day of just how little we as an advanced society really know.

Just think of how much we honor and support these fields of study. Then think about how little money, time, energy, and respect we give to the study of psychic energy. Most of our society pays very little attention to the journey of spiritual awareness.

Psychics do not know everything for the same reason that scientists, doctors, and spies do not know everything. *We are on a journey of discovery*. What we know today leads us to greater understanding for tomorrow. Getting an education in developing psychic awareness is a learning process. Not only does it entail learning about psychic energy, but it also includes learning about the nature of reality. To become psychic, you must transform your definition of what life is. You may begin to see yourself in a new way.

The Psychic Call

Jeff is a computer network engineer, happily married with two children. His sister had a psychic reading with me a few weeks earlier and Jeff was curious to see what a psychic would tell him, so he called me for an appointment. When he came to me for the reading, he seemed nervous and a bit skeptical. When we were nearly finished with the session, I asked him if he had any questions. He anxiously began to tell me that when he was driving his car, just daydreaming or listening to music, he would often have strong feelings or thoughts about family or friends. These feelings, he said, had recently begun to evolve into clear visual images, and he told me that certain scenes would emerge in his mind's eye as if he were observing a dream.

Jeff confessed that he'd been rattled a few months earlier. In an image, he'd seen a friend of his being unexpectedly laid off from his job. Jeff soon learned, a week or so later, that his friend had in fact been laid off. What seemed to unnerve Jeff the most about this incident was that life, he told me, was not what he thought it was. If he could "see" this incident before it happened, he asked me, what then was linear time and free will? Jeff told me that as an engineer he had been trained to think logically and rationally. What was happening to him was not part of the world with which he was familiar.

I have worked with many people who have told me similar stories—people who, without seeking it, have had psychic episodes and breakthroughs. It is not unusual for people to at first ignore these episodes of psychism and then, when they can no longer deny them, to attempt to rationalize a paranormal experience so that it fits into their definition of what is possible. But psychic energy is compelling and persuasive. Those who have experienced what we call the supernatural are rarely satisfied afterward to live their lives solely from the physical perspective. They become increasingly aware of the depth of spiritual resources that lie within them.

When we allow ourselves to investigate the nonphysical world, this investigation eventually leads us into the experience of a broader definition of both life and self. If we continue the search beyond the accepted boundaries, we eventually encounter our spirit, our soul, our being without form. This awareness can guide us into an inner world beyond our imaginings. We exist without restrictions and limitations. This is life teeming with energy, connection, and creative possibility. This is spirit. This is soul.

Intuitive energy and psychic energy have intelligence and beauty. As we evolve and grow, we draw deeper into this graceful energy. Our intuition emerges in our lives, not only to allow to us to access information and give us guidance but also to give us a glimpse into the divine. Our soul is on a journey. As we increase our awareness of the potentiality of intuition, we uncover wisdom and create from Source. Psychic energy rightly used is the gift we have been given that will enable us to connect with vast intelligence and unlimited possibility.

Along the journey of inner knowing, we will be led into the mystery of life. Our search to understand truth will begin to reshape us like a flower that twists and turns itself as it seeks the sun. While working with many people who are developing and exploring intuition, I have discovered that each of us is as unique as a snowflake. Our intuition emerges as individualized as we ourselves are.

We can best appreciate our own intuitive and psychic abilities by becoming aware of how the energy first emerges in our lives. It may be in subtle ways, such as knowing when a loved one is feeling pain. Some people will have unexpected premonitions of worldly events—often tragic events like a plane crash. Others will have dreams of friends and loved ones, dreams that later unfold in life the way they saw they would in the dream. When meeting someone new, most people at some time or another will have "gut feelings" about the new person that are difficult to ignore. It is when we pay draw attention to the small ways that we are guided or given information that we can begin to understand how intuition is uniquely surfacing in our lives.

For some people, intuition and psychic encounters are unmistakable and momentous; it may be difficult to ignore them even though it might be also be hard to understand what is happening. Such experiences may affect not only ourselves, but also our families and friends in surprising ways.

My Psychic Beginnings

From an early age, I remember seeing what I now recognize as angels, animal spirits, and other ethereal visitors. I saw colors and light surrounding people, plants, and animals. In some of the first drawings I did as a child, I outlined people and plants in purple, the color I continuously saw encircling others. I first remember encountering someone in spirit when I was about eight years old. I was riding my bike near an open field, and in the distance I saw a woman walking toward me and waving to me. I quickly rode my bike onto the grass, jumped off, and ran toward her. I was so happy to see her. The next moment she was gone. I looked all over but I couldn't see her. I realized then that I had no idea who she was; she didn't look familiar. Yet I could still feel my joy in seeing her and my disappointment when she vanished. Something in me recognized her and even loved her.

I grew up in Massachusetts, and each year in elementary school beginning in the third grade we would go on a field trip to Salem Village, a restored Puritan town and the location of the infamous witch hysteria of the late 1600s. In between watching women dressed in heavy cotton skirts and white bonnets make candles and apple butter, we would pass the still-standing iron-gated stockade where heavy wooden gallows once were used to keep the witches from "causing evil." We visited the "witch house," where we heard fantastic and frightening stories of women and children who were accused of causing sickness and evil to farm animals and people. I could feel it all, see it all. It left quite an impression on me.

My mother was a missionary and a United Methodist minister. Each night before dinner we read from the *Daily Word,* a book of Methodist religious reflection. We never talked about psychic things. That wasn't part of our religion, never a subject for discussion of any kind. So I never revealed to my family that I could see and communicate with deceased relatives, nor did I tell them about the many dreams I had about events that would later come to pass. I kept to myself the silent, secretive world that seemed to follow me despite my best efforts to deny it.

Most members of my family went on to study religion in school, eventually earning advanced degrees in divinity and religion. But my life never seemed to fit into this mold. Instead, I was focused on trying to understand what was happening to me. Had there been acceptance of psychic energy in the churches and schools that I attended, then perhaps I, like many others, would not have had to endure so many years of shame and confusion.

Yet despite my reluctance to accept and reveal my psychic encounters, and despite my desire to suppress my talent for communicating with those who have passed over, my psychic ability would not be denied. By the time I was a teenager, the dreams, the visions, and the precognitive knowledge of events began to overwhelm me. The more I tried to repress it, the stronger it worked to emerge. I did not see any value in knowing and seeing what others did not see and know. To me it just made me feel different and odd.

My perspective did not began to change until one day when I was nineteen years old. I was riding the city bus and a tired-looking young man took the seat next to me. By his side I "saw" the spirit of an older dark-haired woman. She stood by him while he sat, and clutching her chest, she asked me to tell the man how much she loved him. I tried to ignore her, but she pleaded with me to tell him she loved him. She told me that she had died suddenly and she needed to let him know how much he meant to her.

Reluctantly, and feeling foolish, I asked the man a question about the area, not wanting to blurt out that there was a woman spirit by his side. He told me that he was not too familiar with this part of the city; he had only come this way to go to the funeral of his mother. Extremely nervous and with sweaty palms, I asked him if she had dark hair and if she had died suddenly of a heart problem. He looked at me with an expression of total shock. I told him that I could see her standing very close to him. I told him that she loved him very much. Tears came to the man's eyes and he became quiet. I quickly got off at the next stop, even though it was far from my destination. Eventually it began to occur to me that I may have helped both the man and his mother. I had not previously considered that psychic ability could be beneficial.

It was then that I decided to make a deal with life. If I was meant to be a psychic and help people, then people would come to me without effort on my part. I told God that I would not promote myself or hang the "psychic" shingle over my door. It was up to those benevolent and loving spirits who seemed to be my constant companions to advertise for me. At the time it seemed like a fanciful wish, yet the requests for sessions began to increase significantly.

Now, after over twenty years of giving readings to people as diverse as scientists and goat farmers, as far way as Australia and Iraq, I know the potential and power that the psychic world has to offer. The small private cocoon of psychic knowing that I lived in as a child has blossomed. I have helped many hundreds of grieving parents, family members, and loved ones transform their sadness to peace by relating to them personal intimate messages from their loved ones in spirit.

When we are assured that those we thought we had lost now live on in peace and joy, we can be released from our fears of the unknown. I have also been able to help crime victims and law enforcement officials solve difficult cases by revealing unknown or overlooked evidence. It seems that in every area of life—in relationships, finances, life purpose, health, and career—psychic information has been beneficial and useful. Yet it is not just providing accurate information that has spurred on my career as a medium and psychic. I've also been motivated by the deep joy that I have received from my intimate connection with the spiritual realm and the ability to open the doors for others to experience the wisdom, love, and sometimes silliness the unseen world has to offer. As we develop our psychic aptitude, we cannot help but bump into the spiritual power that we possess. When we realize our divine nature, we become empowered in both the internal spiritual and the external material realms.

The stories in this book are taken from the many encounters that I've had while teaching psychic development classes and workshops, and from private sessions. I have observed how people sometimes timidly and sometimes with courage step into the unknown. My awareness that people approach psychic development through specific innate modalities has come over many years of watching, listening, and encouraging the spiritual and psychic growth of others. I have seen the passion and excitement in those who discover that they have within them the keys to their psychic and spiritual progress.

This book is not just about my psychic journey and the people I have met and worked with; it is about the journey that all of us are on. We are evolving. The unseen is becoming seen. The unknown is becoming known. Though others are still arguing for or against psychic phenomena, I know that it is just a matter of time. Sooner or later, we will arrive in belief and wisdom at the doorway of the spiritual world, a very real and tangible spiritual world. Our senses are refining themselves. We are becoming more capable of perceiving the sublime. As we draw closer to truth, love, beauty, and all things of God, we will begin to know more intimately that we are all one. Our thoughts, our emotions, our choices, and our lives intermingle. We all touch one another. There is no division.

What we call intuition can be our guide into this divine connection with ourselves, others, and God. Our intuition is authentic and genuine. It can lead us into who we truly are. We can experience our essential nature as pure, untouched, divine, and sacred. We can embrace within ourselves the power and magnificence that is the core of our being. The call of psychic energy comes to draw us closer to this truth.

2

WE ALL INTERACT WITH PSYCHIC ENERGY

W̶e are by our inherent nature equipped to keep in constant contact with all of life. We live in a world streaming with energy. We ourselves are streaming energy— flowing, connecting, reaching out to others, and withdrawing into ourselves. What we call psychic phenomena is this very energy, which carries and holds by vibration, intelligence, and emotion. It is the unseen, nonphysical fundamental nature of what is. It is energetic stuff that has already been or is on its way to being physical. We are biologically outfitted not only to connect with the unseen world, but also to build our knowledge of it. Our interaction with the spiritual world never ceases. Even when we are unaware of or skeptical about its existence, we intersect, collide, and respond to the spirit world that surrounds us.

We do not give much thought to the continuous functioning of our physical senses. Most of us have the ability to touch, smell, taste, see, and hear. Whether we are touching a rough surface or a smooth one, we trust our sense of touch and do not second-guess this ability. We accept as reality what we taste and smell, hear and see. Our physical senses are so much a part of us that it would be almost impossible to imagine a life without them.

Our intuitive ability is as natural to our overall functioning as our physical senses—perhaps this is why it is often referred to as the sixth sense. Intuition is integrated into our daily lives as much as our other senses are. Just as our five physical senses interpret the physical world for us, so does our intuition interpret the spiritual world. We use our intuition to discover our personal and soulful truth. It is through our intuition that our purpose as a soul is revealed to us.

With our intuition we learn to navigate the inner worlds and become aware of the spiritual realms. Our intuitive faculty has wisdom and strength. We just access it in a different manner than we do our more physical senses.

Our Intuitive Childhood

As Albert Einstein said, imagination is more important than knowledge.[2] Imagination is one of the ways our intuition communicates to our more conscious self. When we are young, our intuition guides us to create a future that will bring us the opportunity for happiness. Small children dreaming of building houses and roads or singing on a stage are being guided by their intuition to try out various roles and aspects of themselves. Children have the ability to imagine, to play, to create. Through what appear to be fantasy and daydreams, their souls intuitively guide them to choose their paths in life.

As we get older, however, our intuition is often replaced by logic and reason. We muffle the quiet, gentle voice that prodded us to imaginative self-discovery. But our intuition is not snuffed out. It continues to operate, sometimes through mild nudges that we call *coincidence*. We think of a friend we have not seen for years, and then that friend calls us on the phone. We are searching for a particular job and overhear a conversation on the subway or in line at the grocery store about an opening in the kind of work that we are seeking.

When we become more conscious of the small events of our daily lives, we begin to discover the silent presence guiding and assisting us. We become more aware of this part of us. It is natural that we seek out this silent witness, and searching for our truth nurtures our spirit, which is as essential to our well-being as food and water. When we have no dreams or visions of happiness and fulfillment, we can wither into addictions, depression, and all kinds of mental and emotional abnormalities. But the child within us still lives, still thrives on the ethereal.

How Our Intuition Functions

Where is our intuition? We have a nose to smell with, a tongue to taste with, ears to hear with. But what part of us does our intuition use? Is it our brain or maybe our nervous system? Our intuitive receptors are much more elusive than those of our physical senses. Our intuition is a complex and intricate biological function. It begins in the energy surrounding us, which is known as our *aura*. The aura is energy and vibration that is, for most people, invisible to the eye. The aura is an interconnection of energy circuits that are capable of connecting us to the teeming streams of life force all around us.

Our aura is intertwined with our chakras, which are non-physical energy centers that connect us to various levels of consciousness. Each chakra is a vortex of related energy that fuses our thoughts, actions, emotions, inspirations, and potential. The chakras also contain the energy of our past, present, future, our soul's blueprint, and our purpose in this life and as a soul. Our chakras are the doorways our spirit uses to access the nonphysical realms. They connect us to our guides, angels, and to the multitude of spiritual realms.

This complex web is organized by vibration. Each chakra houses a family of similar and related energies. We are a complete multidimensional system more effective than a cell phone or a satellite. We are equipped to communicate with all of life, and with practice we can learn to read and interpret energy. We can also learn to tune into specific energetic information much like we tune to a radio station.

In the physical world in which we live, we primarily use the seven major chakras. I am aware of twelve chakras, yet we have not fully activated and accessed much beyond the seventh. The seven major chakras connect us to the physical world around us and the various realms of consciousness, although we have not yet fully learned how to make use of these multidimensional parts of us. Because each chakra interprets psychic energy somewhat differently, and because most of the time we are more developed in certain chakras, we each receive and interpret the psychic flow of energy surrounding us in our own unique way.

In the seventh chakra, which is located above the head, resides information about our soul purpose, life cycles, guides, and karma. This chakra is usually pure, clear, and reliable in containing the overall design of a person's life. Energy interpreted by our seventh chakra will contain messages from our guides, loved ones, and our Higher Self.

Our sixth chakra, also called the third eye, contains mental energy, thoughts, and beliefs. The sixth chakra is also able to transform energy into vision and thought, and with this chakra we see clairvoyantly. Our intuitive sense of knowing also comes from this chakra.

The fifth chakra, located in the throat, is the chakra referred to in the Bible at the beginning of the Gospel of John, where it states that in the beginning was the Word, the Word was with God, the Word was God. Musicians, singers, professional speakers, and those who teach or chant use this chakra.

The fourth chakra, our heart chakra, receives energy as emotion. Love, serenity, peace, pain, anger, all the feelings both difficult and loving make their way to us through our heart. Our hearts can also receive divine love, and the heart chakra receives intuition as empathy and compassion.

The third chakra is located in our solar plexus. For many people, this is the main intuitive channel. We receive energy through this chakra as "gut feelings." This chakra is often open without our awareness, soaking up the energy of the environment.

The second chakra, located below the belly button, receives energy in a more physical way. Very much like the first chakra, located at the base of the spine, the second chakra responds to our physical world, finances, relationships, and career issues. Intuition received through the second chakra is often in the form of kinesthetic experience and knowing; it can be difficult to put into words what is received through this chakra. The first chakra also grounds us to the physical world, and it is through this chakra that communication with animals, plants, and the natural world takes place.

Our intuition and psychic receptors reach out through our chakras and into our surroundings to interpret information to us in the form of words, images, feelings, and impressions. When we gain enough practice, trust, and knowledge of this energy language, we can accurately interpret not only our own energy, but also the past, present, and possible future of others.

Our Full Potential

Our bodies contain a complex and beautiful web of energetic possibilities. We are multidimensional beings moving more and more toward the awareness of our true potential. Our bodies are equipped to handle the rigors of living in the physical world. As a species we have survived hunger, heat, cold, illness, and stress. Our bodies are also designed to fulfill our spiritual needs, adapting and responding to our soul's purpose through the many challenges of our daily lives. What we have come here to do, our bodies can achieve.

Our bodies come equipped with the ability to know beyond our physical senses. Shutting down, not listening to our intuition has caused us to operate at less than our potential. When we do not use our full range of sensory potential we can become heavy, depressed, and self-involved. Our egos might try to convince us that we are the most important life form, and the only life form with intelligence and worth. When we separate ourselves from the multidimensional stream of life, we can feel lonely and without purpose.

There is inner sight and there is outer sight; there is inner hearing and there is outer hearing. The difference between inner and outer perception is not that one is "real" and one is not. It is that one modality can access the physical world, and the other can access the inner worlds. Both of these modalities have as their tool the physical body. Our bodies can take psychic vibration and translate it into useful information, similar to the way that the ear accepts sound waves, or the eye takes vibration and translates it into color and form. Opening ourselves to accessing information and guidance through other methods beyond our physical senses does not weaken us, but in fact can strengthen us. The energy body that extends from our physical body holds valuable and useful information for our physical and spiritual health and well-being. Our chakras, or energy centers, hold the energy of emotions, beliefs, and the experiences of our lives. They can also access and connect us to healing, loving higher vibrations.

We are at our best when we are going beyond ourselves. Transcendence not only lifts our spirits; it stimulates our capacity to create the lives that we desire. The invisible web surrounding us links us to all the seen and unseen aspects of life. It connects us to the infinite.

3

THE EMERGENCE OF PSYCHIC ENERGY IN OUR LIVES

~~~~~~

It often happens that people who have no interest in psychic or intuitive phenomena find themselves in the midst of an otherworldly experience they cannot explain. This happens to people from all different backgrounds, religions, occupations, and races who are living their lives with no interest in anything psychic or paranormal. Suddenly they find themselves involved in an extraordinary situation that has no reasonable explanation. They may not want it or be looking for it. They may not believe in it.

Sometimes people dream of friends or family, and their dream carries an insight or premonition that might help them. Sometimes people dream of events in the world that later come true. For others, their energy field is like a sponge absorbing the information around them. Often after a death in the family, a survivor will feel the spirit of the deceased person trying to communicate with them. Sometimes a traumatic event opens us up to avenues of spiritual love and help. Or we might be intuitively led to cancel an airline flight or take a different highway, finding out later that we escaped a disaster. If we believe that the presence of a guide or angel may have kept us from harm, we feel comforted.

It seems that Spirit is always operating even when we do not believe. However we are first introduced to psychic energy, we find that a doorway to the inner realms has opened for us, and we begin to perceive the unfamiliar. We don't know why.

This is what happened in Sara's life. Sara is a busy mother of two who works full-time at a busy law firm. She lives in a middle-class community. She drives a minivan. She is the last person you would expect to be talking to spirits and seeing her deceased father and grandmother. Yet in her busy life, Sara takes time to listen to and communicate with the unseen.

A few years ago her father, who had always worked hard and been healthy, died unexpectedly. Sara had always been close to her father and had hoped that he would be a part of her two young sons' lives. After he died, she placed his picture in her sons' bedrooms and spoke of him often, hopeful that her children would know as much about him as possible. Still, Sara was startled when her youngest son, Shawn, laughing and sing-ing one morning, told her that Grandpa was in his room and doing funny things to make him laugh.

Sara wanted to believe that her father was in fact playing with her son, but her more logical thinking wouldn't allow her to completely accept it as true. Shawn continued to talk about Grandpa, and Sara continued to listen. One day Sara, while busily cooking dinner, felt a warm hand on her shoulder and smelled the familiar scent of her father's aftershave. For the first time since he had passed, she felt with certainty his pres-ence by her side. Tears came to her eyes. Then almost imme-diately Sara felt her father's warm laughter, and she started to smile.

Her logical mind is not completely ready to accept that this is truly an encounter with her father's spirit, yet there is no mistaking the warmth and comfort of his presence that she often feels. Sara always assumed that psychic information came to people in the form of a vision or knowing. But as she opens herself to receiving guidance through more emotional avenues such as feeling his warmth and caring, she is becoming aware of her increasing psychic ability.

Sara fears that if her neighbors and some of her friends find out that she not only feels a connection with her father's spirit, but that she has also become interested and involved in developing her psychic abilities, they will think her to be foolish. She has always been an achiever in school and in her career, yet she is finding that her interest in psychic phenomena is becoming the most compelling endeavor that she is involved in.

This seems to be the way that Spirit often works with us. We are living life the best way we know how. We are doing the things expected of us—at home, at work, in the community. We may be doing fine in life, but we lack a sense of adventure and meaning. Then the intuitive life opens a world of exploration and mystery. We begin a spiritual journey that winds through our strengths and our weaknesses. We usually begin the intuitive journey in the known and proceed from there.

Spirit comes to us to activate our growth, to push us beyond our limitations. It also comes as a connection to love, often a love that we have never known. Spirit is not dry and boring. There is intelligence and humor in the universal all-knowing. Spiritual energy and psychic phenomena are a part of the world that many people desire to know more about.

Psychic energy often comes to us in times of difficulty. Quite frequently the psychic world opens for us, revealing a concern and caring that takes us by surprise. In seemingly improbable ways, Spirit intervenes in the challenging circumstances in which we sometimes find ourselves.

Lisa and Clayton

Lisa is a good example. She called me one Monday afternoon. Her voice was faint and shaky as she left a message telling me that a friend of hers had referred her to me and she wanted a reading as soon as possible. She initially wanted my help in investigating an awful crime that she was involved in. When

I met with her and started her reading, I was nearly over-whelmed by the distress, grief, and discord I felt.

Her husband, Clayton, came through immediately and explained to me that his very recent departure into spirit had been quick, unexpected, and tragic. He had died from a gun blast to his chest. I asked Lisa if he had recently passed into spirit from a chest wound. She told me that a week before, an intruder had come into their home. Clayton heard noises from the bedroom and went into the hallway to see what had caused the noise. He then surprised the intruder, who shot him.

As is sometimes the case with traumatic crimes, the information that Lisa wanted came quickly. I felt that the man who had killed Clayton had already fled the area. I felt that he was traveling north, most likely to New York City. I felt as if eventually he would be jailed there on another offense, and then brought back to North Carolina to face murder charges in Clayton's death.

Lisa and Clayton had been married less than a year, and along with Lisa's two other children they had a three-month-old son. From spirit, Clayton described to me the marriage ceremony he and Lisa had had on the beach at dusk. He told me he loved Lisa dearly and thanked her for seeing the good in him and helping him in so many ways. Although he told Lisa that he had work to do in spirit, he would stay very close to her, his son, and his two stepchildren.

As the shock wore off, Lisa sank into a depression and was unable to work. She started to sleep much of the time. It took lots of effort for her to care for her young children, and the grief and loss she felt was always present and unrelenting. She struggled for the next two years.

Clayton and Lisa had shared a dream of one day moving to the beach. During one of our sessions, Clayton encouraged her to pursue that dream. One day soon after, she drove the three hours to the beach, went into a real estate agent's office, and asked to see houses for rent. The first house they went into had been vacant for a few months. The agent told her that if she liked it, she could move in right away.

Lisa told me that when she opened the door and went in, the house seemed large and empty; there were no curtains, furniture, or appliances. The only thing in the house was a kite with a drawing of Scooby-Doo on it sitting on the fireplace mantle. Lisa started to cry, and she told the real estate agent she would rent the house.

Through her tears while she recounted this story, Lisa told me that Clayton had had a playful obsession with Scooby-Doo. He owned Scooby-Doo coffee mugs, posters, and stuffed animals. He even wore Scooby-Doo boxer shorts. Seeing the Scooby-Doo kite in the house shook Lisa out of her lethargy. She soon moved in and felt able to look for work, eventually finding a job as a waitress. Her children enrolled in a neighborhood school, and they began to go forward as a family. Through love and tragedy has come the gentle hand of Spirit easing the painful loss of a father and husband.

∾∾∾∾∾

Whatever our beginning interests have been with Spirit, it is not long before we are surprised and even amazed. Spirit can be playful and wise. Spirit knows us better than we sometimes know ourselves. Intuition development is thus a partnership. Spirit speaks, we listen; we speak, Spirit responds. It is one of the most magical and joyful relationships we may ever have. It is for this reason that many people are driven to become more intuitively skilled. Intuitive development is a process that can open us to laughter and purpose. It can also become an aspect of life that we rely on. Psychic energy is not always abstract and elusive. Many people experience the supernatural very concretely, and depend upon it on a daily basis.

Busta, Kenny, and Iraq

I first met Kenny when he was on leave from duty in Iraq. He was just twenty-three. He had joined the Army at twenty-one and was in the first round of soldiers who were deployed to the Iraq war. I am not sure what spurred his interest in having a session with me. He had never been to a psychic or medium, but he told me that he was open and receptive to what I had to say.

During our session the spirit of a dog came through. The dog was wagging his tail and was eager for me to let Kenny know he was present. I described the dog to Kenny, and he asked me if I was sure that I was referring to a dog that was dead. I felt pretty sure that the dog was no longer living. Kenny said that it sounded like his dog, but his dog was alive and living with his mother. He then told me that maybe it was his uncle's dog that I was connecting with. We went on to other areas of interest in Kenny's life, and then he quietly left. A few days later I received a phone call from him and he told me that after the session he went home to his mother's house and discovered that his dog, Busta, had died. He was surprised and saddened by this turn of events. He told me that it was his dog that had come through during our session.

More than a year later I heard from Kenny's mother. She told me that Kenny was coming home for a visit as he was getting ready to start his second tour of duty in Iraq and he wanted a session with me. Unfortunately, Kenny got lost on his way to our session and we had just a few minutes to meet. With just a brief amount of time Kenny told me that he had two concerns. A good friend of his, a member of his Army unit, had been killed during the fighting, and Kenny wanted to know if I could contact him. Kenny also wanted me to connect with Busta.

It was difficult to connect with Kenny's friend. He had died recently, a traumatic and premature death. His spirit was present but restless. However, Kenny's dog, Busta, once again came through quite strong. Busta was very close to Kenny; I had images of him right by Kenny's side during the many military maneuvers and dangerous combat situations that Kenny had recently been in. Busta was alert, watching for danger and working hard to keep Kenny from harm. I told Kenny this and he smiled.

We finished our session, and I asked Kenny if he had any questions. He said he had just one. He told me that when he was in risky combat situations he would often feel Busta's presence. He told me that at these times he would call Busta's name, and he wanted to know if that would help to bring Busta's spirit closer to him. Kenny was comforted by Busta's presence and wanted Busta to know that he was aware he was with him, guiding him through the danger.

It is sometimes easier for us to accept connection with the spirit world when we are vulnerable and in need. We have bonds with others, including animals, that transcend the three-dimensional world. When we allow ourselves to open and receive the care and nurturing that the unseen offers, we can find a help that we never knew existed.

∾∾∾∾∾

Kenny's experience of what we call the supernatural is straight-forward and down-to-earth. His beloved dog joins him in Iraq. What could be more natural?

Sara's love for her father and her children has created a bridge for them to interact and unite. She is encouraged by her ability to feel her father's presence, and because of this she is motivated to develop her intuitive and psychic skills.

Until her husband's death, Lisa was not very interested in psychic phenomena and she had not given much thought to the paranormal. Now she finds immense comfort in knowing that her husband's spirit is close, and that their young son might also feel his presence throughout his life. Since his death, Lisa has focused on her psychic growth. Her desire to connect to Clayton has inspired her to understand and increase her psychic aptitude. In the process, she has developed her mediumship ability and has become a beacon of light for others who are suffering through similar losses.

The Beginning of Intuitive Development

Each one of these people—Lisa, Sara, and Kenny—has entered into a relationship with the spiritual world, somewhat like adventurers in a foreign land. What they initially will rely on to guide them on this journey are the aspects of themselves that they are already familiar with. These might include their ability to intuit through empathy, thoughts, the gut feelings in their body, or their rich dream life.

Not everyone comes into psychic awareness in the ways that these three people have. For some it will be more subtle— perhaps a book or a television show has piqued their interest. Others may be led by curiosity and a sense of exploration; they look to the psychic world to guide them into understanding the meaning of life and truth. For some it just makes sense— they don't need a reason. For these people, it just feels right to explore beyond the known.

Intuitive development proceeds differently for each of us. We know the difference between a thought, an emotion, an ache in our body, or a prayer. We can learn to recognize the subtle identity of extrasensory stimulus. When we tune into psychic energy, we exercise a part of ourselves that we don't often use. It can be a slight feeling of intensity, or a persistent knowing with no obvious explanation. Psychic energy is engaging and intelligent. It can be personal and intimate. People are often startled by the warmth of the connection they feel with the unseen.

As we focus on developing our intuition and psychic ability, we will be amazed at our skill and shocked at the errors that we make. Being right, accurate, and good at reading energy are not that important at the beginning of this journey. What is more essential is our willingness to be wrong, to take risks. The spirit world loves to help us. All we need is an open mind, the playfulness to use our imagination, and enough confidence to step into the unfamiliar. We need to ask to be the student.

What we find as we develop intuition is that it is more than attaining a skill. We will never learn to "become" psychic. It is, rather, the unfolding of our spirit, the evolution of our consciousness. As we seek within for truth and creativity, we discover the extraordinary. This journey requires growth in all areas of our lives. Many of our assumed beliefs are challenged. We can find ourselves sometimes overwhelmed—and at times underwhelmed—by the changes in our lives.

Spiritual growth goes hand in hand with intuitive development. The idea of our oneness with all of life takes on new importance. The stability of concrete time and space comes into question, and when we become aware of the intelligence and care of a Higher Power, life unfolds in surprising ways. While perhaps we had previously only given lip service to the idea of nonphysical life, it now becomes a reality.

Like all journeys, it is important to know where our journey into the psychic realms begins and what our destination is. Along the way, we will uncover the deep well of our inner power and face the limitations we have allowed to define us.

Our strengths may even become our weaknesses and our weaknesses our strengths. Intuitive development is about our evolution, our healing, and our wholeness.

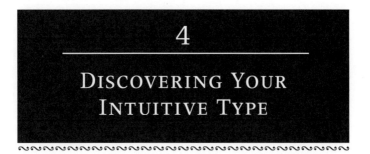

4

DISCOVERING YOUR INTUITIVE TYPE

However we are first introduced to intuitive or psychic energy, we usually attempt to fit it into our comfort zone. For this reason, people approach intuitive development along the path that is most suited to them. There is a Zen saying: *How we do anything is how we do everything.* So it is with our approach to the unseen.

Psychic energy is initially absorbed by our pineal and pituitary glands, and then transmitted through our nervous system. We are stimulated, and nudged. We desire to create meaning for this new energy. Psychic energy runs through us along the pathways that we utilize daily to interpret the world around us. It is similar to how our eyes receive vibration, which our brain then interprets into an image that makes sense to us. So too do we interpret psychic vibrations in a way that we can make use of.

We know, for instance, that people who have witnessed the same accident will often give different accounts of it. One person may recall what the people were wearing or what they looked like. Someone else may have a deep emotional reaction and feel compassion or empathy. Yet another person may analyze the situation and try to understand what happened. We develop and use our intuition in the same way. Without being aware of it, we accept, absorb, and interpret the nonphysical world around us. This is a natural and normal function that happens continuously and without conscious awareness.

While it is not essential to know your intuitive type in order to develop your intuition, knowing how your intuition naturally flows is the path of least resistance, which when followed will lead you into greater levels of extrasensory perception. Most methods of developing psychic and intuitive abilities do not take into account the unique perspective with which we approach psychic energy.

Years ago, when I was in the process of understanding how to harness the flourishing psychic energy that was surging through me, I attended a conference devoted to metaphysical and paranormal phenomena. One of the speakers was a physician who was a forerunner in the study of medical intuition, the ability to psychically tune into the body and describe any illness or disease. He began his session by asking everyone in the audience to take a few minutes and psychically focus on his body to see what we might intuit from it. He told us that he would then describe to us the various broken bones and illnesses that he had experienced.

The room became quiet as we all directed our attention to the tall doctor who stood in front of us. In a minute or two I became aware of a man in spirit hovering close to him. He told me that he was the doctor's father and that he had died of heart disease. With a gentle smile he told me that even though it ran in the family, his son would not suffer or die from heart disease. A few minutes later the doctor interrupted the quiet and began to go through the various illnesses, broken bones, and other issues that he had been through, asking the group to raise their hands to indicate if we had been correct with our psychic impressions. I never got a chance to raise my hand. I didn't see his now-mended broken bones or the other past illnesses that he indicated.

It was not until later in his talk that he shared with the group that his father, who had also been a physician, had died young of heart disease. The doctor had wanted us to clairvoyantly scan his body. Instead, probably due to my more spiritual perspective, I had connected with his father, who wanted to calm his son's fear of a future illness.

I have also never scored well on mental telepathy tests, which measure the ability to receive the mental thoughts of another. These tests usually involve two people—one person holds a card with a particular symbol or other indicator, which they mentally transmit to the other person. The receiver, with an open mind, will usually see an image or have a strong impression of the symbol that was sent to them. This type of test, and variations of it, has been one of the standard indicators used by organizations devoted to researching the existence of psychic ability.

When I participated in this type of test at the Association for Research and Enlightenment in Virginia Beach, instead of sensing the image or symbol that was being sent to me, I received a message for the woman sending me the image about her teenage daughter. Unknown to me at the time, her daughter was going through turmoil with friends and in school. I did not do well on the test, about average, but later when I told the woman what I did receive about her daughter, she asked me to do a short reading for her because she was concerned about the difficult time her daughter was going through. My intuition and psychic ability seems to have a mind of its own. Just as a law of the universe states that likes attract likes, so it is with what we intuit.

If we are emotionally based, our emotions will lead us. If we respond to the world through thinking, we will use our mind in our attempts to understand Spirit. If we are kinesthetic, or based in the physical, we will relate to psychic energy with our body. If we are spiritually inclined, then our connection to psychic energy will be more recognized through essence and sensation.

The emotional intuitive feels energy, and is a natural empath who may experience emotional clairvoyance—experiencing a spontaneous image or impression that is emotionally charged, perhaps with fear, stress, grief, or bliss. Emotional intuitives may also be emotionally telepathic, receiving unprompted powerful emotions that seem to come from nowhere.

The mental intuitive knows, thinks, and sees systems and patterns. Mental intuitives do well with mental telepathy and clairvoyance, the ability to see or intuit an actual image, object, or event.

The physical intuitive interprets psychic energy through bodily impressions or through physical objects, and may excel at psychometry. Psychometry is the ability to hold an object, or view a photograph and receive unknown information about the object or its owner through images, impressions, or physical sensations.

The spiritual intuitive may have visions, see images, and sense the presence of spirits, ghosts, and loved ones dwelling in spirit. They are the type most likely to receive messages from nonphysical beings.

Knowing our natural psychic point of reference can help us understand and better develop our innate gifts and talents. As we grow in intuitive work, our usual preference will evolve and transform, and our ability to realize the full range of our psychic possibilities will blossom.

Types Intertwined

In the intuitive classes that I teach, people often come in believing they have no psychic ability. They think that because they do not have precognitive dreams, are not telepathic, or do not see visions that they have no talent or psychic gift. In order to develop and increase our intuitive and psychic ability, we need to understand ourselves and how we respond to the world around us. Reading energy is more than a mental function. It requires the merging of our energy field with the energy that surrounds us and then integrating with our physical senses. It is a process that engages our total being. As we work with our intuitive and psychic energy, our mind, body, and spirit become aligned. When we know what our intuitive strengths and weaknesses are, we will be able to maneuver our way through the Cosmic All That Is with increasing ease.

Usually, at the beginning of our awakening to psychic energy, we will be aligned with a specific intuitive type. As we travel the path that is most natural for us, before long we begin to experience the paradox of the spiritual/physical world. We are multidimensional beings. On the human, material level we imagine that we live our lives along a linear track. We progress, we change, we grow—one day at a time, one year at a time.

Yet our lives are lived on a soul or spirit level along the turns of a spiral. We have been created from the divine and it is to the divine that we will return. Our intuitive growth winds itself through and into the experience of each intuitive type. We may find ourselves contentedly living the life of the spiritual intuitive, but then our awareness changes, our perspective shifts, and without notice we embrace the sensitivity of the emotional intuitive.

One compelling reason to develop psychic and intuitive ability is that it affords us the opportunity to grow and experience life beyond our self-centered viewpoint. As we do this, we gain insight into our connection to all of life. Consciousness, life itself, unites us. As we grow, the concrete material world that we call home becomes pliable and is affected by our conscious creative desires. It is difficult for us to fully grasp that we create the reality that we experience. With intuitive understanding, we have the opportunity to better appreciate life beyond our personal viewpoint. There is a wise, all-knowing inner guide who calls us to a higher awareness. We begin from our small-self place. Our destination is to fully embrace our greatest potential.

Intuitive Type Questionnaire

The following questions will help you to better understand your intuitive type. These questions are best answered spontaneously as there are no right or wrong answers. There are only preferences. This questionnaire does not rate the degree of your psychic ability; rather, it provides insight into what your natural intuitive preference may be. Remember that most people will be a combination of types.

Knowing your intuitive type provides you with a blueprint or pattern to follow to increase your psychic ability. When we flow with the current instead of against it, we will progress more rapidly and with less effort. The goal of understanding your intuitive type is thus to gain proficiency in psychic awareness, and to develop and enhance your natural abilities.

To better understand your intuitive style, rate yourself on the following observations, using the scoring system at the top of the chart on the next page.

Often=5 points. Sometimes=3 points. Rarely=1 point.

Observations	Often	Some-times	Rarely
1. I experience sudden physical aches or pains when in the company of others.			
2. The feelings and emotions of others affect me.			
3. I have an interest in extraterrestrials, crop circles, or other nonphysical intelligences.			
4. I have dreams or visions that don't seem to relate to anything in my life.			
5. I fail to lose weight, despite constant dieting.			
6. I long for the elevated love of a spiritual soul mate.			
7. I feel I am being taught at night while I sleep.			

Often=5 points. Sometimes=3 points. Rarely=1 point.

Observations	Often	Some-times	Rarely
8. I see streaks or sparkles of light, energy, or color.			
9. I experience anxiety or panic in crowded places.			
10. When I see a loved one suffer, I want to trade places with him or her.			
11. I enjoy discussing spiritual topics and ideas.			
12. I have a strong sense of spirit or soul, but have difficulty with more mundane, day-to-day tasks.			
13. I feel a connection to crystals, plants, or nature spirits.			
14. I feel the presence of God as unconditional love.			

Often=5 points. Sometimes=3 points. Rarely=1 point.

Observations	Often	Some-times	Rarely
15. I want proof or evidence of the existence of psychic phenomena.			
16. I long to be in the presence of divine beings.			
17. I feel I can communicate with my pets or other animals.			
18. I pray for others to feel God's love.			
19. I prefer the words "divine intelligence" to "divine love."			
20. I can see the big picture, but I have a difficult time communicating it to others.			
21. When giving or receiving healing energy, I can feel it flow through my hands or body.			

Often=5 points. Sometimes=3 points. Rarely=1 point.

	Observations	Often	Some-times	Rarely
22.	People tell me that they feel comforted when they are with me.			
23.	I would like a Higher Power to provide me with answers to my questions.			
24.	I had a problem with drugs or alcohol at one time.			
25.	I feel my intuition as a gut feeling in my body.			
26.	People, even strangers, confide their problems to me.			
27.	I have ideas for unique products or inventions.			
28.	I feel the presence of loved ones who are in spirit close to me.			

Often=5 points. Sometimes=3 points. Rarely=1 point.

Observations	Often	Some-times	Rarely
29. I am fascinated by magic and/or spells.			
30. I experience unexplained intense feelings.			
31. I am interested in energy medicine.			
32. I am afraid to be too psychic or intuitive.			
33. I am attracted to different body therapies, including massage, Reiki, and acupuncture.			
34. I forgive others easily.			
35. I enjoy studying mystical teachings.			

Often=5 points. Sometimes=3 points. Rarely=1 point.

Observations	Often	Some-times	Rarely
36. I enjoy studying channeled teachings.			
37. I am interested in shamanism, Native American mythology, and other earth-based traditions.			
38. I desire to be of service to those who suffer physically, emotionally, mentally, or spiritually.			
39. I desire to understand the Universal Laws.			
40. I wonder why I am here, on planet Earth.			
41. I enjoy participating in rituals and ceremonies.			
42. Much of my day and/or week is involved with helping others.			

Often=5 points. Sometimes=3 points. Rarely=1 point.

Observations	Often	Some-times	Rarely
43. I contemplate what the meaning of life is.			
44. I like to daydream.			
45. I spend a lot of time in my garden or in the wilderness.			
46. I feel what others feel.			
47. I enjoy studying the connection between science and spirituality.			

Often=5 points. Sometimes=3 points. Rarely=1 point.

Observations	Often	Some-times	Rarely
48. I live in the present moment.			
49. I communicate with the spirits that live in natural objects like plants, stones, and trees.			
50. My spiritual path is the path of the heart.			
51. I enjoy new technologies and cutting-edge gadgets.			
52. I sense or see spirits and/or ghosts.			

Keep in mind that we all have aspects and tendencies of each of the types within us. We are all a combination of each type. With that in mind, determine your predominant type and your less dominant types.

Add questions		Add questions		Add questions		Add questions	
1		2		3		4	
5		6		7		8	
9		10		11		12	
13		14		15		16	
17		18		19		20	
21		22		23		24	
25		26		27		28	
29		30		31		32	
33		34		35		36	
37		38		39		40	
41		42		43		44	
45		46		47		48	
49		50		51		52	
A=		B=		C=		D=	

If A is the highest sum, you tend to be a physical intuitive.

If B is the highest sum, you tend toward being an emotional intuitive.

If C is the highest sum, you are likely a mental intuitive.

If D is the highest sum, you tend toward being a spiritual intuitive.

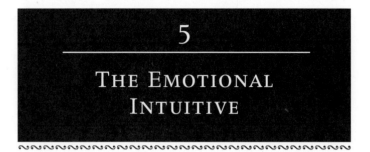

5

THE EMOTIONAL
INTUITIVE

Emotional intuitives travel the path of the heart. They are driven by the desire for transcendental love, connection, passion, and service to others. They are in tune with the soul's quest for a purpose-driven life and for the perfect union, which may be the union of the soul with God, the soul mate, or the twin flame, who is another person or entity that is their soulful equivalent.

While other types of intuitives are also concerned with these spiritual states in varying degrees, the emotional intuitive is the most intensely attuned to this desire. Like all paths, the path of the heart can lead us to divine ecstasy or to human suffering. Emotional states infused with spiritual aspirations can lead to powerful inner experiences and a profound sense of life mission.

Emotional intuitives bring to us the gift of love and a passion to express this love through helping and healing others. They are courageous souls, even though they can be unusually vulnerable and sensitive. They can acutely feel another's pain, and still they desire to heal and to go beyond their personal needs for the benefit others. Emotional intuitives are likely the most giving of all types.

Emotional intuitives can ignite within us the fire of desire, pushing us to unite, search out, and cling to the heart of the divine. Without their energy we might become complacent, self-serving, and not risk our private solitude for soulful union. Their energy is action-oriented; it brings to us healing and transformation. Emotions are temporary, changeable, and fleeting. Emotional intuitives teach us to live beyond our safety nets; they encourage us to risk it all in the quest for love.

Emotional Currents

Emotional intuitives have an innate sensitivity to the emotional states of others. This sensitivity can arouse strong feelings, causing emotional intuitives to respond to others with devotion and care. But emotional intuitives may also be confused and surprised by their reactions, unable to understand why it is they feel a certain way. They may also find that these feelings recede as quickly as they surface.

Because emotional intuitives receive psychic information through their emotions, they are the most prone to experiencing intense, unexplained feelings. Many emotional intuitives, for example, will feel a strong sense of sadness, anxiety, or fear prior to a tragic world event. They may wake up at night, stressed and worried, with no idea where their feelings have come from. They may feel uneasy or uncomfortable about an event, place, or situation, but have no concrete reason why. This is called emotional telepathy, the ability to have a sudden awareness of the pain, stress, trauma, or bliss that another might be experiencing.

Emotional intuitives may also have episodes of emotional clairvoyance, during which they experience a spontaneous image accompanied with intense feelings of dread or grief over a current or future traumatic or disturbing event. Many emotional intuitives learn over time to push such feelings away. They try to shut down to avoid the psychic waves of emotion to which they are susceptible. But emotional intuitives can also experience waves of warmth and bliss. They can ride on currents of love that carry them beyond the stresses of mundane life. These feelings can become intoxicating. The emotional intuitive may seek out the perfect love through a mate, friends, or a spiritual teacher in order to induce these deep feelings.

Through awareness and growth, emotional intuitives can begin to understand and work with their sometimes extreme and unpredictable emotional states, thereby learning to stay centered and focused instead of becoming emotionally weighed down. They can learn to interpret what they are receiving intuitively and then choose to respond with compassion, sending waves of love and caring back out to the suffering world which has called out to them.

The journey of the emotional intuitive is through the heart. It is a journey that leads them through the sometimes saturated and vivid experience of feelings into the maturity of heart-centeredness. Feelings and emotions are powerful. When we allow feelings such as fear, anger, jealousy, anxiety, and worry to dominate our consciousness, we suffer. Emotional intuitives also take in the emotional energy of other people and of their environment. They are usually not aware that this is what they are doing. Their psychic sensitivities are so attuned to the emotional climate that they can feel overwhelmed just walking into a room of full of people.

More than the other types, emotional intuitives need to learn to decipher and name the psychic inner feelings and impressions that constantly flow through them. Because they can feel so much so deeply, they need to become aware of their own emotional energy, as distinguished from the emotions they may be picking up from an outside source. They also need to learn not to define themselves by what they are feeling.

Most feelings are temporary; they come and they go. Despite any emotional state that we may be in, our spirit, our soul resides calmly within. Heart-centeredness is not a state devoid of emotion. It is also not a state that is swamped with emotion. It is the ability to penetrate into the center, into the spiritual core. Our heart is the doorway to the divine, where we can perceive with clarity and wisdom despite the emotional currents running through our day-to-day lives. It is feeling with the heart of God and the qualities of God: peace, unconditional love, wisdom, compassion, and bliss.

Challenges

Emotional intuitives are, unfortunately, the most likely to make errors in interpreting psychic information. At the same time, they rarely make errors when interpreting the feelings and emotions of others. Instead, they make errors because all too often their interpretive abilities are overrun by their concern and their care for others. They strive to help, heal, nurture, and love the sick, the weary, and those who suffer. Learning how to interpret psychic information is not always easy; for an emotional intuitive, it can be more difficult than for the other types. This is because emotional intuitives respond to energy emotionally, and the challenge for emotion-based people is to learn to interpret energy objectively. They must learn to interpret through heart-centered clarity. They can become adept at shifting away from a powerless stance of absorbing emotional energy and into clear awareness.

Claire

Being empathetic and being intuitively aware are similar but not quite the same. Claire is very empathetic. Because of her desire to help others, her friends often ask her for advice and guidance, and she spends a lot of time talking to friends and family. Her friend Samantha, who is lonely and recently divorced, calls Claire often, seeking advice and guidance.

Sensing the longing that Samantha has to be loved and find a partner, Claire often assures Samantha that she will soon meet a man who is her soul mate. Claire tells Samantha that she intuitively feels that this man will be wealthy and share many of her interests. They will be very happy together. Samantha believes that Claire is intuitive, and she feels that Claire must be receiving psychic information. She's sure that Claire is right. Samantha believes her life will soon change, and she is very anxious.

Unfortunately, many months have passed, and Claire's predictions have not yet come to pass. Claire has not intentionally given Samantha information that is incorrect. The problem is that Claire is so empathetic and so acutely aware of Samantha's feelings that she is not reading the psychic information accurately. Samantha's emotional state and Claire's desire to make her friend happy are influencing Claire too much.

It happens all the time. Out of a desire to help, a healer, a reader, a friend gives hope, love, and comfort. But the energy of emotions and the energy of the heart can be very different. The heart sees with an understanding of the journey. The heart can penetrate illusions. It has the ability to move beyond egotistical desire, frustrations, fears, and anger. The heart knows the truth. It can express forgiveness and unconditional love.

We feel a vast array of feelings—sadness, hope, grief, happiness, loneliness, pain, fear, and many more. Feelings fuel our growth and spiritual progress. Feelings are meant to be felt, and then released. Holding onto our feelings can cause us to suffer and become stuck. We should not dismiss or ignore feelings, but we can't define ourselves by them, either.

An emotional intuitive moves through the currents of psychic emotional energy into the heart's wisdom to a maturity centered in compassion and unconditional love. The journey culminates in the clear vision of peace and inner serenity. The connection and union with the divine is the ecstatic love affair of the emotional intuitive.

Louise

Louise is an emotional intuitive. The people she works with in the intuition class feel highly rewarded. Early on, they release their burdens and emotional hurts to her because, without consciously knowing it, Louise will sit next to those in pain and act as a magnet for their emotional healing. In one partner exercise, she received a message from the father of the woman she was working with, a man who had passed over a number of years ago. The message was that he wanted his daughter to forgive him for his selfishness and drinking.

Highly attuned to emotional energy, Louise feels deeply and is empathetic and sensitive. Her intuition is connected to her heart, which leads her to see and feel the wounds in others. She works in a helping profession as a psychiatric nurse for children. She has a natural gift for healing, and people feel lighter just being around her. She has had psychic experiences with angels and guides, who are part of a soul group that assists her in her work here on Earth. Louise *knows* and *feels* whenever a friend or family member is in need or in trouble.

Because of her high sensitivity and the high expectations she has for herself, she can become exhausted and not take care of herself. She is thus unfortunately at risk of marrying or being in a relationship with someone who is emotionally wounded or unhealed. Louise is likely to intuit the emotions of a potential mate, his desire to love and care for her, but she may miss other important characteristics of his personality. Although she is certain that given enough love and time she can heal anyone, if she is not able to make her chosen partner whole and healthy, she is likely to blame herself and try harder.

To come into balance, emotional intuitives need to learn that while emotions are real and powerful, they can keep us from perceiving the truth. All too often, emotional intuitives feel so much for others that they mistake another's pain for their own pain. But we can never truly heal another by accepting their burdens. Divine energy (God, Spirit) is the healer. We are helpers, busy worker bees, but not the true source for another's healing.

If Louise continues to develop her intuition and her emotional empathy matures, she will be more likely to see with the wisdom of the heart. The intuitively wise heart can love without attachment. It can discern and distinguish immature, co-dependent, and selfish love from love that can truly nourish. Louise will honor the flow of unconditional love and compassion that flows through her. She will then be able to draw to herself, as like attracts like, the reflection of divine love in another.

The Body of the Emotional Intuitive

Emotional intuitives can suffer from allergies, chronic tiredness, and adrenal exhaustion, plus PMS and ovary and uterine problems. They all too often pull from their own physical reserves the energy needed to emotionally heal others, and they often believe they are not doing enough if others are not promptly healed. They need to take time to become aware of their own emotions. They need time away, retreat and solitude. But seldom will they take this self-time.

Emotional intuitives and mental intuitives need one another. An emotional intuitive needs to see the big picture and be less affected by others, whereas the mental intuitive needs the love and sensitivity that emotional intuitives generate so easily. An emotional intuitive works through the emotions and passion of the heart, and a mental intuitive can help them to understand the bigger picture.

Mother Teresa

Mother Teresa exemplifies the evolved emotional intuitive. At the age of twelve, she felt God calling her into missionary service. Her desire at this young age was to serve Christ through selfless love and service. She became a nun, and by age eighteen she was teaching at a Catholic high school in India.

Like Prince Gautama, one day she looked out the window. The poverty and suffering that she saw in Calcutta moved her to begin working among the poorest of the poor. Although she had no funds, she started a school for children living in the Calcutta slums. She relied on divine providence to sustain her work and eventually started her own order, the Missionaries of Charity.

Today the Missionaries work all over the world. They provide help to the world's poorest of the poor. Mother Teresa spread love, compassion, and caring throughout the world. Her mission was larger than one small woman could have imagined. She allowed the divine to flow through her heart, and in so doing so she made the impossible possible. Mother Teresa felt that of all the good that we can do in the world, kindness and love toward one another was the highest virtue.[3]

Emotional intuitives heal and lift our hearts. Their gift is their compassion and unconditional love. They reside in a sea of love. They are capable of intense states of rapture, passion, and connection to God. Their highest state is bliss and divine love. It is with this awareness that they have come to the earth. They carry with them the gift of the highest love.

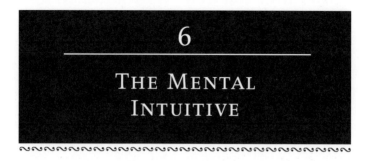

6

THE MENTAL INTUITIVE

For mental intuitives, the psychic spiritual journey is through the mind. This path leads them through the conscious, the unconscious, and then into the superconsciousness—the awareness that leads to divine wisdom, knowing, and being one with the thoughts of God. Mental intuitives have an innate desire to understand. Wisdom calls out to them, sending them impressions, beckoning to them to seek truth above all else. Mental intuitives are constantly being prodded from the depths of knowledge and intelligence. Their challenge is to transform their thinking from ego to enlightenment, to become one with the mind of God. The mind is energy. It is soul. It is continuously reflecting the Divine Spirit through thought, belief, and wisdom.

Mental intuitives are thus attracted to knowledge and have a thirst to know, to learn, to expand their minds. Many are attracted to philosophy, science, and the various spiritual and religious schools of thought and metaphysics. Because their desire is to know, they love to study and discuss theories of creation, evolution, and existence on all levels. Their desire is to know humanity, to know God, to know what is. They are often systems-oriented, and can intuit logic, predict patterns, and perceive the whole. They also love to gather evidence and data to support their beliefs.

Mental intuitives are drawn to astrology, numerology, healing through advanced technology, writing, and inventing. They are naturally mentally telepathic, as they have the gift of being able to receive the thoughts and ideas of others. They are inquisitive and can inspire others to believe and work toward improving conditions and issues on local and global problems. Mental intuitives can also be prophets who foretell the future of cultural, medical, and scientific trends and developments, and are thus drawn to work in these fields. They may be the first to invent or use evolutionary scientific or healing instruments. They may be at the forefront of medical advances. Their minds can be fully tuned to the superconsciousness, absorbing truth and possibility. They are creators of the hope and promise that are advancing us into higher levels of wisdom.

Challenges

The mental intuitive, like all the intuitive types, must work toward balance. When not in balance, mental intuitives can be viewed as geniuses, but slightly nutty, as they might not be able to communicate their ideas and thoughts to others. Mental intuitives can also become overwhelmed by their own thoughts.

When our beliefs are not challenged, when we trust our small self to lead the way, we can create limitations and negativity. It is essential for a mental intuitive to receive thoughts from a higher source. The mind is a reflective pool that can become imbued with divine ideas and enlightened views. The mind can also become a cesspool of limited thoughts and restrictions. A regular meditation practice can be the conduit for a mental intuitive to fulfill his or her potential. These people must also guard against relying excessively on their thought processes. An open mind is much more beneficial than one that is constantly in thinking mode. Being able to quiet the mind and receive divine illumination will bring the mental intuitive to the rich inner garden of inner peace and joy.

For many reasons, mental intuitives are the most prominent psychics and metaphysicians in our culture. Mental intuitives study paranormal phenomena, write books, advance the scientific approach, and argue for or against psychic validity. Working primarily through the sixth chakra, mental intuitives can be strong intellectuals and visionaries who can predict and intuit the future better than most of the types. They are in tune with the vibration of knowledge past, present, and future, along with the ageless wisdom of the higher realms. They may quickly receive insight into how to solve problems and issues that plague the planet. It is not unusual for a mental intuitive to have an instantaneous knowledge of the universal laws and the connections between science and spirituality.

Mental intuitives are often driven to manifest their ideas and visions in the physical world. They can have wonderful visions of events, odd inventions, even advanced cultures and technologies. If these ideas are infused with the energy of unconditional love and harmony of the emotional intuitive, they can be of true benefit to the world.

Karen

Karen is a professor of mathematics at a prominent university, a respected and admired author and researcher. In her private life, her interests include studying the paranormal and taking classes and workshops on spiritual and metaphysical topics. Her approach to intuitive development is to first grasp intellectually what she is to do and then proceed. This method works well in science; however, it is not always helpful when developing intuition.

In a recent class, I had people work with a partner. They were to meditate together, create a bubble of light and love surrounding them, and then listen to any messages or impressions they might receive for their class partner. Karen worked very hard at this. Her brow was furrowed as she focused on light and love. The problem is that we cannot *think* love; we must *feel* it. We can perceive the presence of light through the mind, but the heart must also feel it. Understanding that the heart has intelligence is not a mental concept but rather an experience, and sometimes a mental intuitive will focus excessively on data and information and miss the direct impact.

Karen has become one of the most skilled intuitives I work with. Surprisingly, this is not only because of her natural mental brilliance or her tough-minded approach. Her intuitive emergence was instead fueled by the four cats and two grandchildren that she loves and cares for. Her heart has opened. She now has the synthesis of emotional and mental energy she needs to fuel her spiritual development.

Just as an emotional intuitive needs more mental energy to find balance, so does the mental intuitive need the emotional connection. In intuitive development classes, an emotional intuitive and a mental intuitive can make quite a comical pair. I will sometimes pair them up. They look at each other with wonder and disbelief, yet if they work together long enough, the combination of energies can make them an effective, balanced team.

Unfortunately, many mental intuitives can get too caught up in trying to prove or disprove a theory or idea and miss the true gift of Spirit. Love, compassion, an open heart, and inner knowing are the fruits of intuitive development. Outside proof is useful, but it cannot substitute for the experience of Spirit.

Ray

Ray is one of the most intelligent people I have ever met. When you talk to him, you can almost see his mind at work. He understands the wisdom and knowledge of ancient cultures, dynasties, and mystery schools. He has studied Atlantis, the ancient Egyptian cultures, extraterrestrials, and the written channelings of higher teachers, and he is interested in acupuncture, dowsing, new inventions, and healing technologies. He is engaged in proving the existence of ghosts and life after death. I first met Ray when he came to me for a reading. Like many mental energy readers, he was concerned with the accuracy of the information. He wanted proof. He wanted me to give him undeniable evidence of psychic phenomena, proof that fit into his definition.

Ray reads energy with his mind. He is likely to intuit patterns and make predictions based on these patterns. He likes numbers and math, even directions. When Ray took one of my intuition development classes, he sometimes struggled to accept the kind of intuitive information he received. While working with a partner in one class, he related to her that he felt the strong presence of love surrounding her. He went on about how he could not be sure who or what this love was, and then he struggled to define the source and its content.

We all sat amazed as his mind went to work to understand the love, instead of just feeling it. As he shared his impressions with his partner, tears came to her eyes. She told him that she felt it, too. She hadn't felt this much love in a long time. Ray was initially uncomfortable because he did not recognize the value in his perception of love. As he continued to listen as others shared, he gradually became aware of the transformative power of love. It began to make sense to him. He saw people opening up and sharing their pain and struggles. He knew that this sharing would lead to openness and healing. He initially came to class wanting to learn all that he could about intuition. He was ready to study, to be taught, and he wanted to know how it all worked. Instead he *felt*, and his intuition began to flourish.

Because mental intuitives have the natural ability to make all the parts work together, they are very important for our advancement and evolution. Without them, we simply will not grow as a culture or as a positive world. Because they love the challenges of problems and solutions, mental intuitives can move us forward like no others can. While emotional, spiritual, or physical intuitives can become depressed and overwhelmed on the earth plane, mental intuitives are likely to become motivated. They can overcome obstacles and blocks with surprising ease. But they also can be misunderstood and their contributions overlooked, and sometimes they can get so much information that they cannot effectively communicate it to others. They can also overdevelop their thinking at the expense of other aspects and dimensions of awareness.

When fully integrated, mental intuitives will not only be able to connect with higher levels of wisdom, they will also be able to effectively teach and influence others. Mental intuitives can have a profound effect on the world, since they tend to be sturdy and strong and they like to share their insights and perceptions. Unlike the more sensitive emotional intuitives or the elusive spiritual intuitives, mental intuitives can be unaffected by opposition and proceed with confidence, trusting in their power and ability despite prevailing political, spiritual, or global beliefs.

The Body of the Mental Intuitive

Someone who reads energy through the mind is likely to be prone to muscle tension and stress. They might also suffer with panic, anxiety, insomnia, headaches, and sinus issues. The mind overloaded with energy may also inhibit decision-making and direct experience. The sixth chakra, located in the head, can become overstimulated and overworked.

Mental intuitives tend to be hard on themselves. They can place unrealistic expectations on what they can accomplish, often pushing themselves beyond what is reasonable. Physical exercise can help mental intuitives unwind and clear out their thoughts and reduce stress. They will often have a difficult time sitting in meditation. Their very active minds can find it hard to settle down in silence. They will therefore benefit from a more active meditation, such as yoga or quiet walking in nature.

When mental intuitives become out of balance, they can feel isolated and undervalued. They can contribute so much and at the same time they can feel so little self-appreciation. They need love—spiritual love, romantic love, the love of friends and family. This is their balance, to give and to receive through the heart, but that can seem so indulgent to mental intuitives. Why feel, they ask, when you can contribute in a *real* way? They also can get hooked into finding proof, and the need to believe something is true only if it makes sense to their minds.

Mental intuitives are on a path of transformation of consciousness, and their task is to open their minds to divine illumination and to fuse their individuality with the all-knowing of God and to become one with Divine Mind. Because their thought processes can be so well-developed, mental intuitives must discipline themselves to become open vessels receiving the finely tuned, soothing vibrations from the higher mind, instead of just recycling their own thoughts and biases. Their greatest gift, the mind, is their path to spiritual freedom and realization. Along the way, they may prod us, astound us, even provoke us to new levels of knowledge. Mental intuitives are always leading us to greater understanding and awareness of the world that we live in.

Albert Einstein

Albert Einstein is our shining-star example of a mental intuitive. Born in March 1879, Einstein was the theoretical physicist widely regarded as the most important scientist of the twentieth century. He made momentous contributions to quantum mechanics, statistical mechanics, and cosmology, and he authored the theory of relativity. In 1921, he was awarded the Nobel Prize in Physics. Einstein was and is world famous, which is unusual for a scientist, and his name is still synonymous with genius and extraordinary intelligence.

Although Einstein was raised in a Jewish family, he did not consider himself religious in the traditional way. He did not believe in a personal god. He believed, instead, that there was a creator god that set the universe in motion. He felt that the universe is governed by a set of laws. Of his personal religious beliefs, he once said:

> *A knowledge of the existence of something we cannot penetrate, our perceptions of the profoundest reason and the*

most radiant beauty, which only in their most primitive forms are accessible to our minds—it is this knowledge and this emotion that constitute true religiosity; in this sense and this sense alone, I am a deeply religious man.[4]

While addressing the issue of science and religion he said, "I maintain that cosmic religious feeling is the strongest and noblest incitement to scientific research."[5]

During the course of his career as a physicist and scientist, Einstein was always motivated by a desire *to know*. He sought to understand the universe and to bring this knowledge to others. He opened the door to mystery, and his work was the base upon which quantum physics was built. Here is something else he wrote:

I am convinced that He [God] does not play dice. The most incomprehensible fact about the universe is that it is comprehensible.[6]

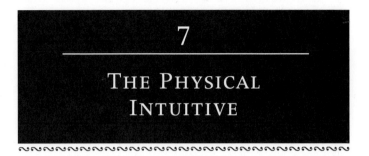

7

THE PHYSICAL INTUITIVE

The physical intuitive is attuned to the vibration of the divine made physical. Physical intuitives are able to experience what is holy, good, and of truth through their connection with the natural world. Physical intuitives often become involved with earth-based religions and spirituality; they bring to us the vision of heaven on earth. Many physical intuitives hold a strong inner knowledge of the earth and her creatures as divine, and they are often devoted to healing the earth. They may be involved in rescuing animals and saving the forests and the seas, preserving all of God's creatures great and small. Physical intuitives see the divine in all of life and give us the gift to see and be in the presence of God. They are able to perceive the divine in a line of clouds and sun, a field of grass, or in the call of an owl through the dark night. They bring us to our senses. They say, "See, feel, wake up. God is here." They are the earth's special ones.

While a spiritual intuitive yearns for the beyond, the physical intuitive knows that there is no need to go anywhere else. Physical intuitives have a quest to let us all know this as they connect with Spirit through the tangible world. They use their senses to access intuitive information more than the other types, and their challenge is to become conscious of essence and pure Spirit. Because their vibration is usually attuned to the physical—which is a denser, heavier energy—their progress in spiritual evolution may be slow, and they can at times have little motivation to explore the higher realms. It is not that they reject the spiritual; they may simply lack the ability to always understand and perceive it as "real." Pure Spirit without form may be a theory or concept.

Injury and degradation to the earth and her creatures motivate physical intuitives to work tirelessly. They may be drawn to transform their local environment, or they may focus their efforts on a global level. When inspired, they have at their disposal the tremendous energetic resources of pure Spirit, which they can transform with little effort into the physical realm where they are capable of healing the body, the earth, and all of her creatures. Physical intuitives' communion with the natural world is often direct and uncomplicated, but unfortunately they may not always be able to articulate what they are experiencing. Like the spiritual intuitive, the most profound contribution of the physical intuitive may be not be through words but through touch or other forms of nonverbal communication.

Physical intuitives are often highly kinesthetic, and they offer healing through direct energetic connections that bypass thought or emotion. Many physical intuitives become adept at hands-on healing, acupuncture, chiropractic, and traditional and herbal medicine. They may be natural shamans and communicate with the spiritual energies of plants, animals, and ancestors. They may also delve into the world of magic, paganism, and witchcraft. They understand the powers of the four elements—air, water, fire, and earth. They can be instinctive alchemists with the ability to perceive elemental energy moving freely through the Devic kingdom, understanding nature in all its complex forms. They have a natural ability to work in unison with, and draw power from, the natural world.

Dorie

Physical intuitives do not always believe that they are intuitive or psychic. Because they pick up energy through their senses and their physical bodies, they often disregard the intuitive psychic energy that rushes through their bodies. Dorie took part in a large intuitive workshop. After one of the intuitive group exercises, she shared that she felt frustrated with her lack of intuitive ability. Other people were sharing their insights, visions, and psychic impressions, but she said she saw nothing, had no revelations, and felt intuitively deficient.

I pressed her to recall any sensations she might have had and asked her to try and recall anything that she might have felt or received during the meditation visualization. With a embarrassed look on her face, Dorie finally told the group that the only thing that happened is that her wrists and hands began to ache with sharp shooting pains. That was all. What Dorie did not know was that the woman who sat next to her had been in a motorcycle accident earlier that year and had gone through numerous operations to repair the many broken bones in both of her wrists. She recently had surgery, where many pins were placed in both wrists, and she was still in constant pain.

Sharon

It is essential for physical intuitives to learn to strengthen their energy field and clear their chakras. One way to do this is to practice self-talk and self-awareness. It can also be helpful for a physical intuitive to develop body talk, which involves asking questions of the physical body. For instance, Sharon works in a busy office. She often works late into the evening, doing her best to complete difficult projects. She has a co-worker whom she sometimes overhears talking on the phone to her husband. Sarah, Sharon's co-worker, is in an unhappy and difficult marriage and often comes into work tense and upset. Sharon would like to help, but she minds her own business and does not intrude into Sarah's private life.

But Sharon has many aches and pains. She is overweight and suffers from chronic tightness in her shoulders and neck. Because of her desire to help Sarah and because of her physical intuitive nature, Sharon absorbs the stressful energy in the office. She has absorbed into her body not only the stress that her co-worker feels, but she has also absorbed intuitive information about Sarah's future. Sharon intuits that Sarah will be harmed by her husband. She cares about Sarah, yet she knows that there is little she can say or do to change Sarah's path. This is how intuitive information can get buried in the physical body. It is energy—information that we intuitively receive but do not know what to do with or how to release. Do we share our gut feelings with others? Do we send them healing energy? Do we offer advice to those about whom we receive impressions?

Emotional intuitives absorb emotional energy, which they may experience as unexplained, intense feelings. Physical intuitives are less likely to take in the emotions of others, but they will instead experience baffling aches, pains, and fatigue. Physical intuitives absorb intuitive energy for different reasons. Usually they are unaware that they are doing it, but they have a desire to help others and do not know any other way to effectively deal with their intuitive nature. The more aware that physical intuitives are that they are absorbing others' energies, the healthier they will be. Unconscious energy from others can make us sick, overweight, and cause us to feel physical pain.

Physical intuitives like Sharon need to jump over the hurdle of belief that tells them they are not intuitive. Just because they don't get visions, dreams, or clear messages does not mean that they aren't picking up lots of information. They are.

Body Scanning

Physical intuitives can practice daily body scans to help them discover when they are absorbing the energy of their environment.

Sharon can learn to sit quietly and scan her body from the top of her head down to her feet. As she does this, she can become aware of any place in her body that feels sore, tense, or tight. She can ask questions of the tension, such as: "Is this my stress or someone else's?" "If the stress or tension had a voice, what would it be saying to me?" "Can I release this stress to the light?" and "What do I need to do with this energy to heal and shift it into unconditional love?"

Answers to these questions will provide insight and provoke deeper awareness of how the body is responding to the environment. The body of a physical intuitive has a high degree of intelligence. Dialogue with the body can bring surprising intuitive information.

Physical intuitives often have the ability to hold an object and read its energy. Personal items that we wear or hold, such as rings, watches, or even car keys absorb our energy, and a physical intuitive is often able to put this energetic vibration into words. As Sharon began to become more aware of how she was intuitively responding to others, she discovered that she had this ability. She had never felt intuitive or gifted, yet she can hold an object or look at a photograph of a stranger and give surprisingly accurate information about the object or stranger.

Martha

Martha grew up in a strict religious family that attended a Baptist church. Although she has worked for many years as a bank teller, her real love is being in nature and communing with animals. She works for the local animal rescue organization and opens her home regularly to abandoned dogs, cats, and birds.

In addition to her two dogs and three cats, she has housed stray pets for as long as two years. She regularly goes on vacation to the ocean and the mountains, and as her children grow older, she hopes to be able to one day move to the mountains and start a new life there. She feels a sense of peace and connection in the natural world.

Martha first came to see me because she felt that there was something wrong with her. She told me that she had a loving family, a good job, and regularly went to church, but still she felt empty, dull, and uninspired. She wondered if she might be depressed.

When I began to read Martha's energy field, I was surprised at the number of animal spirits that work as guides for her. Their love for her was impressive. They spoke of the deep well of love for the earth that existed within her, and they communicated to her through me that there was nothing "wrong" with her. I told her that she was witnessing her beloved Earth being ill-treated and this was causing her psychic and spiritual pain. As we continued the reading, tears started to well up in her eyes. She told me that the neighborhood where she had lived for so many years was growing and changing. New homes, condos, and strip malls were being built close by. She watched the construction—the trees being bulldozed, the smell of burning vegetation, and the constant roar of heavy machinery seemed to be never-ending. She was experiencing a deep sadness over this that puzzled her.

As we worked together, Martha began to express a depth of wisdom that surprised me. She has a vision of universal love and peace, and she knows so well what this earth can truly be. It pains her to see suffering and pollution, and she longs for what she calls the spiritual earth, which, she believes, exists side by side with the earth that we pollute and treat with contempt. On the spiritual earth, all is still pure, vibrant, and sacred.

As Martha began to uncover her spiritual path, her search for her truth led her to study medicinal herbs and hands-on healing. She feels the plants speaking to her and guiding her to help others. She has become a gifted healer. Her natural intuitive style of connection to the earth is a wonderful gift that gives hope and wisdom to others.

The Body of the Physical Intuitive

Physical intuitives can soak up energy like a sponge. Because of this, they may have problems with weight gain. As the energy field absorbs what is in the environment, the subconscious translates this heaviness into physical weight. In addition, the aura will eventually become overburdened with the added energetic stress that surrounds it. A physical intuitive is most likely to bring environmental energy into the body, whereas a mental intuitive will channel it into the mind and a spiritual intuitive will lift energy into higher awareness.

Emotional intuitives will feel and connect through the heart, but physical intuitives soak up psychic information in their bodies. As a result, they have difficulty knowing when and what they are picking up from outside of themselves. Because their intuitive energy is centered in the third chakra, or solar plexus, they are more likely to absorb the energy into the stomach and lower organs and may suffer from chronic skeletal and muscular illnesses. Chronic fatigue, arthritis, and fibromyalgia also plague many physical intuitives who have over time absorbed the energy in their surroundings. Physical intuitives tend to respond well to herbal medicine, homeopathy, chiropractic work, massage therapy, and any other therapy that assists them in integrating subtle and invisible energies.

As physical intuitives develop and grow spiritually, they can learn to absorb divine love and light instead of the energy of their surroundings. The body can actually become a conduit of the divine. Physical intuitives can spiritualize the body with more ease than any other type. Their journey is to harmonize heaven and earth, and so their bodies can be the channels through which spirit becomes flesh.

Within the physical intuitive is a vision of the perfect earth. This is not a whimsical, storybook revelation; it is the essence of our perfection. It is the secret that we have searched for throughout the ages. Physical intuitives hold the key that will bring forth perfect health, agelessness, and eternal life. These are buried deep within every physical intuitive, and their task is to call forth their power, to insist that we listen, hear, and respond to the earth with sacred care. Physical intuitives knew thousands of years ago when they saw the beauty of the planet that this is the home of the divine. It is time once again for the physical intuitive to wake us, to guide us to this truth.

Dr. Edward Bach

Dr. Edward Bach, a well-respected British physician, is an example of a devoted and accomplished physical intuitive. In the 1930s he became driven to discover a simple way to heal the body using nature in its most pure form. He relied on his intuition and his natural healing abilities to guide him. Using the essence or the vibration of plants and flowers, he developed a method of healing that is now used in over sixty-five countries by individuals and respected medical professionals.

Educated at the University College Hospital in London, Dr. Bach was an accomplished physician, surgeon, and pathologist. Even though he had a lucrative general medical practice in London, he became dissatisfied with the orthodox methods of traditional medicine, which he felt did not treat the whole person.

Eventually he left his medical practice determined to find a new way to treat people suffering from disease and illness. He felt that a new system of medicine, a more holistic approach, could be found in nature. He was motivated by his previous study of homeopathy and sought to discover a gentler form of natural healing through the use of plants and flowers. He traveled through fields and meadows, observing and intuitively listening to the healing properties of plants and flowers.

It came to him that he could bring balance to the emotions and aid in healing the physical body through just the essence of a plant. He saw the dew that settled on the leaves and petals, and he felt that it could absorb and transmit the plants' healing properties. To determine if he was correct, Dr. Bach used his own body as a laboratory by first experiencing the emotional and mental state that he wished to address. He then treated himself with various combinations of his flower essences, until he felt himself restored to health and well-being.[7]

Dr. Bach left the world with a legacy of intuitive insight into the genius and simplicity that nature has to offer.

Mary, Mother of Jesus

Another exceptional physical intuitive is Mary, the mother of Jesus. The Bible reveals little information about Mary. We know that she was a descendent of David and she was related to Elizabeth, mother of John the Baptist. The Bible tells us that before marrying Joseph she was told in an angelic vision that she would give birth by miraculous conception to a son who would reign as the son of God. We know that she traveled to Bethlehem to give birth to Jesus in a manger. The Bible does not tell us the role that she played in the education and ministry of Jesus. We are told in the gospel of John that she attended the crucifixion of Jesus.

When the Dead Sea Scrolls were discovered in 1947, they revealed more insight into the life of Mary. According to these ancient documents, Mary was an Essene. The Essenes were a community of men and women who dedicated their lives to understanding the inner mysteries of spirituality, living lives of purity, and triumphing over evil in the world. Some sources believe that Mary's birth into the Essene society was prophesied and anticipated as a holy event. Her birth, the prophecy foretold, would lead to the emergence of Light within the darkness of the world.

Within the Essene community, Mary was very much loved and revered as the woman who would one day give birth to the Holy Master. She dedicated her life to serving the wisdom of God, consecrating herself as a vessel for the divine. She lived a life of beauty, simplicity, and purity, always aware of the great gift of miraculous conception that she was to receive.[8]

Mary, mother of Jesus, holds the energetic blueprint for the physical intuitive. Physical intuitives live with the inner vision of the divine made physical; they are able to perceive that within form lies the seed of perfection. Symbolically, the virgin birth suggests to us the interplay and interaction between the human and the divine. The veil that we believe restricts and separates us becomes nonexistent through Mary; she conceives from the formless, then creates pure form. What we experience as physical and material extends itself from the womb, the dark, the void.

While pregnant, Mary travels with Joseph to a distant town and gives birth to Jesus in a modest barnyard setting. For the physical intuitive, the spiritual is not so much in the ethereal, the elusive, or the intangible; it exists in what we can see, touch, and feel. The Light passed into and through Mary, making its home on the earth, creating the pattern for spiritual-physical perfection. For many physical intuitives, the earth is the soul, the receptive, and the Mother. The earth, the physical, absorbs and reflects the light of the heavens and glows from within with the warmth of soul, nurturing our whole being, body, mind, and spirit.

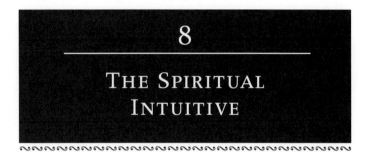

8

THE SPIRITUAL INTUITIVE

Spiritual intuitives draw their strength and power from the intangible world. Drawing upon their tremendous supernatural resources, they give us the gift of transcendence, the ability to rise above the mundane. They offer us a glimpse into the cosmos. They know better than others that this world is temporary, and they wait and yearn for what lies beyond. Spiritual intuitives live in the world of cause and effect with the memory of perfection. They can soar with the angels and converse with the divine. They call us into our highest spiritual knowing.

The journey of spiritual intuitives is that of enlightened freedom. They are learning to live in the midst of duality with the awareness of oneness and non-being, unattached and unencumbered. Their home is beyond the skies; they are here in the physical world as visitors.

More than any other type of intuitive, spiritual intuitives are able to live in the present. They have a natural tendency for spontaneity and can quickly immerse themselves in the experience of bliss, ecstasy, and pleasure. They often do not have a planned agenda, goal, or destination, but are here to experience *what is*. Not the *what is* of this world, but the *what is* of eternal truth.

Unfortunately, spiritual intuitives can have difficulty managing daily life. Because they are attuned to no time and live primarily in the present, they can have trouble with the more routine aspects of life such as paying bills, showing up on time, and keeping track of paperwork. Where a mental intuitive finds meaning and mystery in patterns and trends, the spiritual intuitive may rebel, feeling restricted and limited by the probable. Spiritual intuitives want freedom and openness. They want to be able to shift, to change like chameleons. They are not attached to form of any kind. To the spiritual intuitive, what you see is temporary and not what you will get. Reality is without form.

Psychic Gifts

Spiritual intuitives often have rich dream lives. In their dreams they might travel to distant locations, communicate with those who have departed the physical world, or visit mystical realms.

Because their spirit frequently rises into the etheric currents, they are likely to have precognitive dreams and visions, which they might not always be able to understand. They are also likely to enjoy astral travel, which is the ability to send the consciousness and soul-self outside of the physical body to distant places.

Especially when they were young, many spiritual intuitives have had encounters with spiritual beings such as loved ones who have passed over—ghosts or spirit entities and guides. Spiritual intuitives are often able to see and communicate with the spiritual realms in a natural, matter-of-fact way.

Spiritual intuitives are likely to be attracted to energy work such as Reiki and healing touch. They also enjoy toning, chanting, and deep trance work. Because they work well with others, you will often find spiritual intuitives in groups. They take naturally to community, tend not to be ego-centered, and they often seek out spiritual teachers and leaders. Unless they find this community and a sense of belonging in the world, they can become lonely and lost.

Spiritual intuitives do not naturally bond with the physical. They need to seek out an identity and a purpose to give meaning to their lives. This means spiritual intuitives can have a difficult time using their intuitive gifts in the world of the here and now. Many spiritual intuitives will tell me that they do not know why they are here on earth. Some have told me that they feel as if there has been a cosmic mistake; they feel they belong in the beyond, peacefully soaring the cosmic currents.

Janice

Janice has devoted most of her life to her spiritual pursuits. She can spend hours immersed in celestial pleasure. She loves to tone, to chant, to meditate, to spend hours with her spiritual friends in spiritual workshops and classes. She enjoys helping others through quiet meditation, and she feels as if she connects and receives intuitive energy that can uplift them.

She is often frustrated, though, when it comes time to share what she has experienced, for she often has very little that she can verbally express. She sees colors, mostly purple and gold. She remembers sparkles and streaks of light. Although she is frequently at a loss as to how to share these experiences through words, a look of quiet contentment on her face reveals the depth of her spiritual experiences. It is not unusual for her to see auras around people, plants, and animals, and she sometimes sees images of people in mirrors that are not there physically. In her dreams, those who have died and her guides give her messages. Spirit is a reality for her.

At times the prospect of living in the physical world leaves Janice depressed. She is not sure why she is here and what will give her life meaning. The physical world sometimes seems slow and heavy, while the world of spirit is enchanting and magical. For this reason, the monastic cloistered life has always had an appeal for her, and she feels that she has lived many past lives as a nun, a monk, or a devotee. This lifetime is very different for her; she is forced to achieve an inner equilibrium and balance the demands of the world and a powerful inner life.

An emotional intuitive is drawn into the world to heal, help, and love. A mental intuitive desires to figure out systems and to understand how, when, and why things occur. A physical intuitive is at home in the world. Spiritual intuitives, however, often do not have a strong drive to connect with the world. They might even be inclined to find ways to escape it through alcohol, drugs, or other addictions. Long periods of fasting, meditation, or spiritual pilgrimage also appeal to them. While, like all types, spiritual intuitives do have a mission, a purpose for being in the physical, they can have the hardest time finding out what that mission or purpose is. Spiritual energy can be elusive, intense, and seductive. At times, a spiritual intuitive would rather reside in the higher realms.

Many spiritual intuitives find a sense of peace and connection through writing, channeling, and working with sound and spiritual healing. They can bring us the gift of the higher vibrations. The experience of spiritual energy can be light, warm, and energizing, but bringing this higher vibration into the physical can be exhausting work. This is one reason why spiritual intuitives can have difficultly in grounding their gifts and natural talents.

The Body of the Spiritual Intuitive

Because spiritual intuitives access intuition more outside the physical body than the other types, they can experience elevated states of ecstasy and bliss, only to plunge into deep despair and indifference. They can also suffer from headaches, dizziness, and a lack of physical vitality, and if they do not establish a meaningful connection with the physical world, they can become depressed or apathetic. Because they intuit through their higher chakras, their seventh and higher chakras are highly developed. Their challenge is to pace themselves and live in the world of matter.

Some spiritual intuitives suffer from attention deficit disorder (ADD); their consciousness may quickly flit from one thing to another. They may be like butterflies, only needing to lightly touch and observe ideas, objects, people, and thoughts in order to absorb their energy. They then drift away, freely moving wherever the breeze may take them.

Spiritual intuitives may also experience thyroid and other glandular issues. Part of the function of the thyroid gland is to regulate how energy is used by the body. The pituitary and pineal glands accept spiritual energy, the adrenal glands generate fuel for the physical body, and the thyroid receives energy from both of these glands and works to regulate and nourish the physical, mental, emotional, and spiritual systems. The spiritual intuitive may not, however, always know how to use the rich storehouse of available spiritual and psychic energy, and this failure can manifest in glandular and endocrine system imbalances.

When energy has no path for expression, it can become static and overcharged. Spiritual intuitives can thus benefit from the physical intuitive's natural ability to ground and use energy through the body. Massage therapy, healing touch, and yoga can help the spiritual intuitive come into balance. Career counseling, dream analysis, and breath work may also be helpful.

Corina

Corina is a lovely soul. She dreams of faraway places and supernatural beings, and she has visions of past and future events. Easily immersed in her inner experience, she spends time each day writing down her dreams and other psychic impressions. Most of her family has passed into spirit. She feels them close to her and communes daily with the spirit world.

Corina is a spiritual intuitive. Unlike physical, mental, and emotional intuitives, she is more attuned to nonphysical energy than the energy of others or her environment. She can become so overwhelmed with energy at times that it is difficult for her to make sense of what is happening to her. She can also have difficulty getting her needs met in the physical world. Her biggest struggles are finding her place, her home in the here and now.

While she is very talented, she has not had steady work in a long time, and she is worried about her financial situation. She has a difficult time understanding how something like a job and a schedule can ever fulfill her. While she longs to be in an intimate relationship, she also longs to be in the bliss of pure spirit and spends as much time as possible there.

Her challenge is to ground herself. She has to learn to live in the routine of day-to-day life. Highly spiritual people such as Corina can suffer greatly if they do not learn to balance the spiritual with the physical, but many do not want to do this because it's not much fun. Learning moderation is not very exciting work, especially if you can be soul traveling or visiting higher vibrational frequencies. This is sad, because spiritual people have so much to teach us. They come as teachers, as guides who can (better than others) show us the reality of other worlds. Their wisdom is immeasurable. But before spiritual intuitives can manifest their gifts in the physical world, they must be able to see the value in the mundane.

Corina would love to have a meaningful job. She has taken many classes in all kinds of subjects. She has started and left college a few times. Her struggle is that she tends to be easily bored. She prefers spontaneity and wants the freedom to respond to what comes her way. Without this freedom, she feels trapped and restless. She is, however, working on integrating the awareness of her spirit into her everyday activities. She knows this task is necessary, but it is not very rewarding.

When Jesus encouraged us to "be in this world, but not of it," he was speaking the language of the spiritual intuitive. As spiritual intuitives become better able to respond to the demands of the physical world, they will find that their intuitive ability will also increase. It is not that they become more intuitive; it is that they are better able to channel their intuition into usable information. They will be able to share their inner experience of light, radiance, and illumination with the outside world. Spiritual intuitives will find that they will then be fulfilling their true mission of bringing their soul and others' souls into oneness. They will shed the boundaries of the physical division that previously limited them. Bliss is their spiritual path. They have come to live in oneness of mind, body, and spirit.

Spiritual intuitives guide us into the timeless. They tend to be accepting, nonjudgmental, and accommodating souls who have come here to learn patience. They dwell among us with the secret of the heavenly realms always whispering and calling to them. But still they are here, lifting our awareness to the stars, to the Light, soaring freely with the angels.

Edgar Cayce

Edgar Cayce was an extraordinary spiritual intuitive. Although he died over sixty years ago, the advice, wisdom, and guidance that he gave to others, documented in thousands of psychic readings, still to this day influences the study of metaphysics, psychic phenomena, soul development, knowledge of health and well-being, and our understanding of the world we live in.

Cayce has been called a mystic and seer, and he is often thought of as the best-documented psychic of all time. For over forty years, by simply lying down and closing his eyes, he was able to put himself into a self-induced hypnotic state in which he was able to access information, wisdom, and guidance that transcended the limitations of time and space. From this relaxed state he responded to questions from people all over the world. His breadth and range of wisdom and insight was limitless. He answered all types of questions, from "How can my son heal from leukemia?" to "What is the meaning of life?" to "How did civilization begin?"

Edgar Cayce was born on a farm in Kentucky in 1877, into a strict Christian family of modest means. He sought to make his living as a photographer, but in his mid-twenties he accidentally discovered his unusual psychic talent, and a life beyond his imaginings began to unfold.[9]

Though for the most part uneducated, he gave detailed and valuable advice to people suffering from incurable and complex medical conditions and illnesses. Although his initial readings were health-related, he before long began to emphasize the importance of our connection to our souls and to Spirit. A common theme of Cayce's readings is that Spirit is the source of all life. He believed that our soul's quest toward union with God is our most important task in life. He also felt that everyone is capable of attuning themselves to the spiritual realm and discovering our oneness with all of life, and in experiencing this truth becoming free.[10]

The A. R. E., the Association for Research and Enlightenment, headquartered in Virginia Beach, is a spiritual organization devoted to the ideas and principles of Edgar Cayce. Every year it attracts tens of thousands of people from all over the world. The over twenty thousand readings that Cayce did during his lifetime are still studied, examined, and discussed by seekers everywhere who hope to gain important insights into living purposeful, healthy, and spiritual lives.

The Buddha

The Buddha stands as the pinnacle of the spiritual intuitive. His life and teachings have brought the world into the spiritual realm—not as random, inconsistent phenomena but through meditation as an attainable conscious state.

Prince Siddhartha, better know as the Buddha, was probably born sometime around the year 563 BCE. It was predicted at his birth that he would be a great king or a buddha (an enlightened one). He grew up in the midst of great luxury because his father wanted him to become a king; he did not want him to enter the spiritual life. For this reason, the king kept the prince close to the family and the material world.

Although the prince married young and lived contentedly within the palace, in his late twenties Prince Siddhartha experienced three situations that changed the course of his life. While out hunting with several friends, he met a person who was in grievous pain, a person who was incapacitated by the effects of extreme old age, and he then observed the funeral observances for someone else. These experiences led Siddhartha to contemplate the suffering of others, and he grew increasingly aware that there was no escape from the endless rounds of life and rebirth that he and others were bound to experience. The prince became aware that he was not able, even from his high station in life, to bring peace to those who lived lives of desperation and pain.

Through these inner revelations, in what Buddhism calls the Great Renunciation, Prince Siddhartha left the palace, abandoned his life of luxury, and embarked on life as a seeker of truth. He sat under the legendary Bo Tree in contemplation, then traveled to the abodes of holy persons. Despite his contemplations, travels, and numerous severe austerities, the prince did not consider that he had made worthwhile progress during seven years. He had, however, become known to others as Sakyamuni, the Sage of the Sakyas.

Prince Siddhartha concluded that the life of austerity he was living was not leading him to divine awakening. He continued to sit and to contemplate. Then one day, still sitting under a great, spreading Bo Tree, he felt that he was beginning to undergo profound and extensive realization and awakening. It is from this time that Prince Siddhartha began to be referred to as the Buddha, a title implying his having gained enlightenment. Prince Siddhartha Gautama, the Buddha, is said to have attained nirvana in association with this enlightenment experience. Nirvana is a state in which suffering is eliminated through the abandonment of desires, which are the cause of suffering. The attainment of nirvana is held to bring release from an otherwise endless succession of reincarnations or rebirths.

The Buddha teaches enlightenment, the realization that God can be attained through meditation. His awareness of the spiritual life led him to renounce material riches and strive to live fully in spirit and teach others the way. The Buddha taught us how to live in spirit, even when we are bound to the physical. He lived and taught that to find peace in life one has only to look within. The world, he said, only leads one to increased suffering. His teachings have brought this message to millions.

His legacy of communion with Spirit thrives in the world today. He accomplished and taught the daily practice of meditation as a way to bliss and oneness with the godhead.

> *The Way is beyond words and expressions, is bound by nothing earthly.*
> *Lose sight of it to an inch or miss it for a moment,*
> *And we are away from it forever more.*[11]
> *"Seek something which death cannot destroy."*[12]

9

DEVELOPING YOUR PSYCHIC GIFTS

~~~~~~

E ven though intuition will initially surface in different ways for the four major types, we all can develop our intuitive potential in similar ways. The first step is to understand our innate intuitive modality. When we are aware of how intuition naturally flows through us, we begin to notice more and more instances when we are receiving psychic impressions. Whatever we put energy into will increase and expand. We will also gain confidence and be better able to proceed rapidly in our psychic growth.

Intuitive awareness is more a process of spiritual unfoldment and discovery than it is acquiring a set of skills. When people come to intuition development classes, their intent is usually to learn how to become *psychic*. They would like to be able to know more. They want information about their career, love life, and family, maybe their health. We approach intuition to add to our lives.

Yet in the intuition development classes that I teach, I used to begin with an exercise that very quickly showed people how psychic they really were. I didn't exactly trick them, but I would bypass their logical minds and access their intuitive knowing before they knew what they were doing. Attendees would be surprised by their ability to be accurate in their psychic impressions. As time went on, however, intuitive ability would decrease instead of increase. What I have come to realize is that it is not our intuitive ability that is lacking. Rather, it is limited self-understanding and lack of spiritual identity that keep us from accessing our true nature. Our soul needs neither help nor techniques to become psychic. Our intuitive nature can unfold naturally. Most people use their intuition in one way or another in their everyday lives. They may not call it intuition, but just as our other senses cannot be eliminated at will, neither can our intuition.

Many people are constantly open to and receiving intuitive impressions. It is important to become aware of when and how we are intuitive so that we will be better able to understand and then make the most of this ability. Also, if we are in a continual receptive state, we will at some point become overwhelmed and burdened with too much energy. We may also begin to have experiences that are confusing and disturbing. In both these scenarios, we will eventually shut down, which is not optimal because when we deny and repress our intuition, it manifests and emerges in ways that usually do us and others no good.

Active Listening

For this reason, it is essential to accept our intuitive nature and begin to work with it. I recommend that people take time each day to just sit and be silent. We seldom feel comfortable with our ability to *meditate*, so I suggest just being quiet and listening. It can be helpful to begin the quiet time with a few deep breaths. As we inhale and exhale, thoughts and emotions surface. The thinking mind will chatter and carry on. This is perfectly normal. Just keep breathing. Listen for the quiet space between and underneath the mind's constant activity. In this quiet space, allow whatever happens to happen.

Active inner listening is similar to prayer and meditation. Active listening is a state of calm, alert awareness. It requires self-discipline to be alert to the inner voice. Our thoughts and emotions tend to grab our attention. Practice listening, and then make notes on whatever surfaces. Write down any sensations, thoughts, feelings, smells, or images that surface, but merely record them; do not try to make sense of them. When you are finished, put away your notes. The purpose of this practice is to begin to train your intuitive self to use this time as its outlet. With consistent practice, your intuition will begin to respond positively. As time passes, more images, feelings, and impressions will surface.

I suggest that people begin meditation with a prayer of protection. We have domain over our energy fields. If we ask for white light, and only to receive what is our and others' highest good, then the universe responds to our requests.

Initial Phenomena

When we first begin to consciously open to psychic energy, we can experience various kinds of phenomena. Regardless of your intuitive type, there are some commonalities.

Many people will initially see purple, indigo, or white light. This often indicates the opening of the third eye, which is located in the sixth chakra of the forehead. There may also be a feeling of pressure, random flashes of light, or other images. Psychic seeing can be quite different from our physical sight. Images similar to cartoons, photographs, or random images may appear. Some people will see unfamiliar faces, one after another. If this happens, focus on the breath, breathe deeply, and they will pass.

Our imagination is an important tool that helps us to understand the meaning of what we are experiencing. It is our imagination that works to interpret and to help us to make sense of energy. Through practice, we will begin to understand the patterns in our inner symbology. Do not get too attached to what emerges. If it is important for you to know something, the information will keep returning in various forms until you understand it.

Often there will be no obvious sensations or feelings at the onset of intuitive development. The mind may wander and drift. We think about what to make for dinner, or we get bored and discouraged. This is normal, and it eventually gives way to stronger inner currents. We may also resist opening to what we do not understand. Our strong thinking mind may respond with fear and distrust to this new way of being; often, if our mind rejects becoming quiet, then the psychic energy may surface in our bodies. This is common in classes. After an exercise, some people will report in frustration that nothing happened for them. They received no impressions, no feelings, and no images.

However, when pressed they will share an ache or a pain that they felt intensely during the exercise. After the exercise, the feeling or ache usually disappears. If this happens, breathe into it and imagine that you are moving the physical sensation into your conscious awareness. Eventually you will experience the energy through an emotion, a thought, or an image. A physical intuitive is the most prone to receiving information like this through the body.

Interpreting Psychic Energy

Learning to interpret psychic energy is like learning another language. Initially, making sense of the feelings, images, and impressions we receive can seem confusing and overwhelming. With practice and over time, however, patterns begin to develop and we become better skilled at discerning the meaning behind what first appears to be random stimuli.

Psychic energy can be very subtle, but it is persistent. At first, it is best to focus on the quiet. Most likely, what is obvious and loud is not intuition. When we are beginning intuitive development, if large chunks of information surface they are most likely not true intuition but rather the thinking brain at work. We cannot open a book in another language and immediately read it. It is highly unlikely that, without time and attention, we can easily understand intuitive information. Intuitive work can also be exhausting, especially at the start when we exert the most focused attention. It is a part of us that we are not used to employing, and so we have to align our psychic receptors with a part of our brain that we rarely use.

Discerning psychic sensations, symbols, images, feelings, and sounds requires patience and persistence. For this reason, it is important to share our impressions with care. We have to train ourselves to be clear receptors.

Accuracy and Clarity

To read energy clearly and accurately, it is necessary to move through our inner blocks and obstructions. When we repress or deny emotions in ourselves, we will likely read them in someone else. This is called psychological projection. Our intuition is not an escape from such emotions, such limiting beliefs and internal obstacles. Our growth will be accelerated through intuitive connections, but we are still responsible for making positive choices and following through with action. When we repress and deny our need for growth, we can project it onto others. When we do intuitive work these projections will surface, and they can cause confusion and pain for other people.

A client of mine, Cindy, is a massage therapist. Cindy feels that when she is working on her clients, she intuitively picks up information on their emotional and psychological wounds and pains. She has a client, Jared, who she feels had a wounded past. She feels that when she works on him, she becomes aware of his unresolved pain. One day after a session with him, Cindy shared her impressions of his past wounds with him. He was not receptive. She was confused as to why he did not accept her intuitive impressions. When she spoke to me about this, she could not understand why he was not more open to her offer of help.

Often, the feelings we pick up from others are not theirs but our own. Whenever we pick up pain, wounds, and strong feelings from others, it may be that those feelings are repressed within ourselves. Unless someone asks and wishes to share difficult and painful feelings, it is important that we not intrude on their privacy. It may be more useful to ask ourselves if those feelings we attribute to others may exist within ourselves.

It is also important to share our impressions of others *only if they ask*. We sometimes get intuitive feelings or dream of others, and we feel compelled to let them know what we have received. Why else, we say, would we be receiving information? We must have something of importance to tell them. Psychic energy surrounds us at all times. It is like the sun in the sky. If we are outside on a cloudless day, we will most likely receive the sun's golden rays. It is the same with psychic currents. They surround us. We cannot be where they are not.

If you feel that you have important guidance to share with someone, ask for divine direction. Ask for the divine to intercede. The person you have guidance for will usually ask for your opinion or bring up their concerns to you. They will open the door for you to share the guidance you have received for them.

10

PSYCHIC PROTECTION

~~~~~~

The interpretation of psychic energy is most accurate and helpful when we are attuned to the energy of the Light. The Light can be described as a vibration of pure electro-magnetic energy. It is radiant and luminous. It is omnipotent, omnipresent, everlasting, and is not affected by time and space. The essence of the Light can be present in varying degrees in all matter—at any time, in any shape, size, or manifestation.[13] After passing out of the physical body, we are given the choice to merge with the Light, a vibration of cleansing, healing, and forgiveness. When we do so, we surrender to our divine nature and the power of a supreme consciousness; as we do this, the individual soul willingly releases its negativity, anger, and unhealed ego-centered aspects.

Choosing the Psychic Source

Reading the energy currents of the ethereal plane and lower energies can be seductive, for we are given information and guidance that for a while may be accurate. But then the guidance that we receive begins to be inaccurate or unsettling. There are, unfortunately, lower vibrational energies that are confused and will draw people in by psychic phenomena as a way to gain power and control.

If we go into psychic work wanting to have power over others or to use the energetic currents for our own manipulative purposes, we will draw to us such fragmented and confused discarnate beings and negative thought forms, which will try to influence and use us. There are all kinds of obstinate energy forms that refuse to go to the Light.

For various reasons, some people who pass over view the Light as a place to stay away from. They may feel as if they are undeserving, or they may want to hold onto their physical identity and become ghosts that still inhabit the physical world. In order to do this, they need our energy to stay in this denser vibration, as they no longer have the energetic makeup to do this on their own. They would love to attach themselves to us, but unless we are under the influence of drugs or alcohol, or unconscious due to an accident or surgery, it is very difficult for them to penetrate our aura.

True possession by negative fragmented spirits is rare. What is more common is that we attract discarnate thought forms and confused souls who are operating under their ego-driven illusions. They have no ability to control our thoughts, emotions, or behaviors. It is more likely that they will influence the intuitive information we pick up, leading us to feel fear or doubt and be bewildered by what we receive. The divine always expresses through the constructive and the affirmative. We will feel uplifted when the energy that we are connecting to is from a divine and positive source.

I once had a client ask me a question: if someone wanted to act in a harmful or negative way—perhaps kill his wife, or lie, steal, or cheat—would a spirit guide help him? This client wondered if Spirit always works toward the positive.

There are many thought forms or energy forms that exist on different levels of reality. Based on our soul, thoughts, emotions, and intent, we attract to us energies that are the most similar to our own. Unfortunately, people who have a desire to create misfortune for others or to harm themselves will attract similar energy forms. This is one reason I am against the death penalty. We should keep a destructive spirit determined to cause pain to others in a body for as long as possible; for once such a spirit is released from the physical body, it can, if it desires, attach itself to another body or mind and find a way to influence others who, like itself, have negative aims. Ultimately, we have been given the freedom of choice. This extends into the spirit world as well as the physical world.

The exception to this rule is that once a soul has entered the Light, it cannot return to the etheric, more physical energetic levels and create or promote harm. The Light is a vibration that elevates our consciousness to a higher awareness of love and truth. We no longer dwell in the toxic pool of ego-driven emotions, thoughts, and beliefs. We are connected to unconditional love and forgiveness.

While we are engaged in intuitive or meditative work, the Light also keeps us safe and free from any negative and harmful influences. When our intention is for the highest good for ourselves and others, confused or defiant energies cannot influence us in any way.

Light and Darkness

In the summer of 2005 I was asked by a detective with the Raleigh, North Carolina police department to help in an investigation of a three-and-a-half-year-old unsolved murder case. During the few weeks that I worked with the detectives, I had the opportunity to go with them to the apartment complex where the murder took place. We did not enter the apartment where the crime had been committed. Instead, we stayed in the parking lot and surrounding area, which was a well-populated area of apartment complexes.

Even though many months had passed since the crime, the area still had the energetic imprint of the traumatic murder. The detectives were very anxious to solve this crime, and so for a few hours they questioned me and pushed me for as much information as I could psychically access. The most difficult part of this was the disturbing quality of what I had to connect with. In addition to raping and killing this woman, the man who committed the murder had killed another woman. He was addicted to pornography, his thoughts were caustic, and I had to touch and feel my way through all of it to give clear and accurate information.

I have worked on other murder and criminal investigations, but none have been as disturbing to me as this one. At one point, as I sat in the back of the detectives' car, I told them I needed to take a moment to pray. I was feeling overwhelmed and I needed to feel the presence of Spirit. As I did this I experienced a rush of what I can only describe as mercy and compassion for the man; I was surprised by the intensity of it. I knew that finding him would give him the opportunity to seek redemption, and I felt that Spirit was reaching out to him.

In the same moment I told the detectives that I knew where the man had lived at the time of the murder. I led them to another adjacent apartment complex, and as we drove by the buildings it became clear to me which building had been his and that he no longer lived there, although he was still in the area. From this and previous psychic information that I had been able to access, the man was identified, given a DNA test, and arrested a few weeks later.

In proportion to the darkness that I felt during this investigation, there was the equal presence of Light. I felt safe and protected even though the influence of what felt like evil was palpable.

In life we can, and usually do to some degree, experience negativity and stress. Although our soul is always pure and intact, we often operate from the parts of ourselves that are not fully healed. Yet we have the ability to choose which aspect of our being we reside in.

Clearing the Energy Field

Part of taking care of ourselves involves becoming aware of our environment and how we allow others to affect us. We tend to be psychically and unconsciously adversely affected by others' thoughts and emotions. When we are around people who are negative, angry, depressed, or fearful, for example, we can absorb these emotions from such people. Intense feelings form energy clouds that can cling to us. For many people, the third chakra acts as a funnel where they receive others' energy, usually unconsciously. We cannot carry someone else's anger, fear, or stress and resolve it for them. We only feel what they feel, and suffer physically, emotionally, and spiritually.

Many women and some men tend to absorb energy from others. The more we understand how our energy field operates, the better we will be able to protect ourselves from picking up negative and destructive energy. Some very loving, helpful people reach out and willingly accept others' hardships, stress, and emotions. When we are aware that we are here to be of loving service to others, it can be difficult not to want to help lift another's burden in any way we can. We can thus fool ourselves into believing that carrying another's pain is good for them and not harmful to ourselves.

Unfortunately, when we attempt to take away someone else's pain by absorbing it, we only trap it in our own energy field. Then we have two people in pain, and because that to which we give energy will expand, the pain is magnified. I have met wonderful, loving people who are constantly and physically affected by someone else's energy. Stomach pain, weight gain, fatigue, lack of focus, persistent muscle aches, and lack of vitality are often signs that your energy field is overburdened.

Many loving, caring people suffer from being natural sponges for the emotional pollution of their environment. They feel the energetic heaviness and are overwhelmed by the responsibility. If you feel excessive guilt, worry, or stress for others, you might, without realizing it, be soaking up energy that is harmful to you.

We cannot absolve or dissolve what someone else has created. While we all desire to be understood, when we take on another's energy we can become drained and confused. If we want to be helpful to others, it is much better for them if we visualize them in the white Light of love and compassion. Intuition is the ability to be aware of and translate energy into useful information. It is not necessary to take the energy of another and experience it as our own. Consider the way doctors and health care practitioners relate to an ill person. They seek to understand and direct others to health, but they would not be effective if they became so attuned with the illness and the patient that they could not lead them through the illness and back to health. Intuition demands that we align ourselves with a higher knowing, a higher compassionate love. Our perception must be centered in Divine Spirit. Then we can help others to experience, through our awareness, perfect health, abundance, forgiveness, and divine wholeness.

This awareness extends into both our environment and our relationships. We may be responding to and absorbing energy from our workplace, friends, schools, and home atmosphere. We do this because we learn as children to fit into the environment of our family. We adjust to the beliefs, habits, and emotions we find, and become accustomed to accepting that the reflections of who we are can be found in those around us. As we grow older, we keep this same pattern intact. Without knowing it, we adjust ourselves to fit into our workplaces, neighborhood, and relationships of all kinds. If our environment is emotionally or spiritually toxic, then we still unconsciously connect to it. In order to be free and choose whether or not we want to connect in this same way, we need to become conscious of what we are doing.

Psychic protection begins with awareness. We initially make contact with our environment through our chakras. When we enter a meeting at work, a social situation, or even a restaurant, our chakras send out energetic antennas to check out our surroundings and connections. We will be drawn to those of like energy, as we will feel more comfortable with those with whom we share a similar energetic makeup.

We are being forced to evolve, since we cannot afford to connect and pull in the toxicity of this world and still remain healthy and strong. Our umbilical cord, though physically non-existent, still exists in its psychic form and keeps us locked into the belief that we are dependent on our limited and competitive-oriented environment. When we continue over time to operate in this way, we grow more out of touch with our spiritual nature. When we begin to identify more and more with our divine nature, we will find that those who are stuck in negativity will naturally fall away. Others who feel and sense the light that flows from us will be drawn near.

One of the greatest lessons we have come to earth to learn is how to care for and love one another. All healing comes from God. The Divine Spirit resides within the soul of each one of us. God alone knows the truth for each individual. We cannot replace God's wisdom with human logic. When we think that we can take another's pain, loneliness, or suffering, we are robbing them of their opportunity to experience God's grace. We are also robbing ourselves of the experience of the divine within. When we become aware of the power of Spirit, we will know that we can trust the working out of our affairs and others'. We will see beyond the forms and appearances to the truth. We will give to others not from a desperate need to fix and control but from the warmth of unconditional love.

Loving and detaching often seem to be at different ends of the spectrum, yet to love others we have to be able to let go of our expectations of who or what we think they should be. We can never really know what others have come here to learn and experience. To keep our karma clear and free, we need to be able to bless and witness what we do not always understand. To be able to love another with the highest love we have is to be able to release another to their choices and decisions. To be a wise psychic or effective healer or intuitive, it is necessary to find the source of love and wisdom within yourself. When we give ourselves over to the care of Spirit, the miracle of the divine expressing itself in our life begins.

If we are personally involved and dependent, then our psychic impressions will be clouded by need. In order to be a clear channel for divine guidance, you have to be able to walk alone on the spiritual path and love without expectation. Loving as an expression of a full, abundant heart will create a river of blessings for yourself and others. This is the way to love that can free yourself and others. It has nothing to do with pain, expectation, control, and security. When we can be with another for the joy and freedom love offers us, we have found the way to true love and oneness.

Truth and Illusion

One of the most important aspects of intuitive development is the ability to distinguish truth from illusion. It has been said throughout time by sages, seers, and teachers that our world is an illusion. If this is so, then it is easy to understand why we would have difficulties in discernment. It is not always easy to see beyond the outward form or the illusion of the material world and into truth.

There is temporal truth and there is absolute truth. I am a woman with red hair who is five feet, eight inches tall. While that is true today, in eternity it is only an illusion. What I really am is a soul, an aspect, in truth the substance of God. This will be true today, tomorrow, and forever. We need to set our anchor in eternal truth, in aspects of God. Love, creativity, abundance, beauty—these are aspects of God. Part of intuitive evolvement involves stripping away whatever is not truth.

Our progress in intuitive growth is in part dependent on our ability to detach from our personal wishes and desires. Our ability to be unbiased plays a big role in how clear and accurate our intuition may be. Even when we feel that our intent is good and spiritual, we still need to be cautious.

We do not like to discuss the shadow side of spirituality. We want to believe that all that we read, hear, and witness in the name of God is of God. Yet we all contain a shadow side. Many of our spiritual practices contain aspects of delusion. Our shadow sides are fueled by our fear-based emotions. It is our shadow that tries to dismiss our inner experiences of Light as imaginative fantasies. It is the shadow in spirituality that fore-casts future destruction and suffering for everyone but those who believe as we do. Whenever we are drawn toward fear and the belief in death, it is the shadow in action. It has been said that this world is the shadow of the divine. In our earth world we will always encounter duality, the light and the dark.

Whenever we have a desire that encourages us to believe that we are better than others, we have entered the shadow. There is delusion along this path. It is tempting to believe that our spiritual path, beliefs, neighborhood, city, and country are better and more enlightened than others. But whatever creates division and separates us from others will eventually weaken us. When we are not mindful that we are one with all of life, even with those people who do not believe as we do, we weaken our bond with the truth.

Gail

I have seen Gail once a year for a few years. She is sixty-two years old and frustrated, she told me, because she does not feel as if her life has started yet. She is unmarried, works full time as an insurance adjuster, and lives in an apartment. In her as-yet-to-be-lived life, by contrast, she is married, has no financial concerns, and lives in a tropical climate in a luxurious home. She told me that for years she has been told by psychics that this would be the life she would be living. She wants to know why these predictions are so far not coming true.

Here is another aspect of the shadow. We take little or no responsibility for what is happening in our lives. We expect the universe to act upon us, not realizing that we create from within. Gail has lived most of her life being cared for by her family, then by her husband, and then for years after her divorce by her alimony. Now she imagines that God will step in and take care of her in the manner that others in her life have done.

We have to be willing to work with the Creator. When we open our mind, our heart, and our soul, then we will be inspired from within to act as a co-creator with the divine. In the shadow life, we have no power, but in the Light we coexist with God. We listen and act upon the guidance that comes from within to create the lives that we desire. We work in unison with a Higher Power by experiencing the God within.

Illusions, shadows, and ignorance can keep us in a fog of confusion. But remember that the shadow is just a shadow with only the illusion of energy and power, and the shadow is necessary for our development. If we did not know darkness, we could not know the Light. In order to find out who we are, we need to find out who we are *not*. As difficult as our failures and disappointments can be to go through, they often open doors for us that we would not have otherwise chosen.

Along our journey to self-knowledge, we have to shed many masks. We have in part identified ourselves by what our family, friends, enemies, culture, and environment have told us is true about us. We have made our choices based on this self, yet this conditioned self is simply a mask that hides us from our authentic self. It is often through what seems like failure that we will often be led to know the true power that resides within us.

Intuitive development helps us to know ourselves and others, not only from our human eyes but from the deeper well of reality. Intuition is, in part, the ability to perceive the world through the lens of the divine.

11

GUIDED MEDITATIONS

〜〜〜〜〜〜〜〜〜〜〜〜〜〜〜〜〜〜〜〜〜〜〜〜

One way to increase our intuitive and psychic ability is to practice meditation. It is in quiet listening that the inner intuitive voice can be heard. Each intuitive type has strengths and weaknesses. The following meditations and visualizations address the area that each type most likely needs to develop in order to come into their full potential. When our type is out of balance, we will not be able to make the best use of our intuition. Physical intuitives, for instance, instead of recognizing that they are absorbing the caustic energy of their workplace, go home exhausted and depleted.

These meditation visualizations provide a framework for bringing the body, mind, and spirit into harmony. You can record these meditations in your own voice and then listen to them in a quiet room where you will be undisturbed. You can also read the mediation a few times, get the general idea, and then close your eyes and trust that it will surface as you need it. It is best not to have any preconceived ideas of what to expect during these meditations. Going into them with an open mind and allowing the experience to unfold for you will yield the best results.

Throughout these meditations and psychic development exercises, I use the word *see*, as in, for instance, "You will see a place in nature." I use this word in the broadest possible way. Many people will not visually see an image, or if they do it may seem made-up or cartoon-like. This is fine and does not indicate your psychic aptitude in any way. Some people are visual but not everyone's intuition will surface in this way. You may not visually see an image, but instead feel it, sense it, or even just somehow know it. Go with what happens for yourself and feel free to use your imagination.

Our imagination is an important tool in psychic development. The difference between whimsy imagination and psychically connected imagination may take a while to discern. Imagination that is psychically connected to energetic phenomena is similar to a dream in that we will be more the observer or participant of it rather than the creator. It has energy of its own.

We do not have to work to make things happen. Although for the purposes of these exercises it may be helpful to begin with your active imagination to kind of "prime the pump," eventually you will be able to know, sense, feel, or see when you are connecting to tangible objective energy.

Emotional Intuitive: The Lighthouse

Because emotional intuitives are usually highly attuned to psychic emotional energy, it is necessary for them to become skilled at balancing with calm insight the feelings and emotions they intuit. When emotional intuitives are able to identify the emotions they are picking up on, they will be better able to interpret what they are psychically receiving. They will then be able to release what they do not need and come into inner harmony. If you are an emotional intuitive, the lighthouse meditation will help you to learn how to accept the emotions that you intuit without being overwhelmed or negatively impacted by them.

- Lie or sit in a comfortable position that you can stay in for a period of time, perhaps twenty or thirty minutes. Close your eyes and take a long, deep breath. Send the energy of your breath to any part of your body that is sore, tense, or tight. Breathe in again, then exhale any stress or tension you find anywhere in your body. Breathe in again and let go of any thoughts, worries, or concerns of the day, or week, exhaling the stress and tension. Breathing and relaxing, going deeper and deeper into relaxation, breathing in, letting go of any emotions that surface, breathing in, letting go, and going deeper and deeper into relaxation. Relaxing, going deeper and deeper into relaxation, releasing any worries or cares of the day—let them go as you breathe out, breathing and letting go any emotions rocking around inside. Let yourself become aware of them and then release them with your breath: easy, calm, relaxed breath, free and easy.

• Imagine that you are on a beautiful beach on a warm and clear day. Imagine that you are walking along the shore, feeling the sand warming your feet, as you continue along the shore. Breathing in the salt air, you feel even more relaxed. The sun is setting as you walk along the shore and watch the waves rolling in toward you. You hear the sounds of the sea, relaxing and inviting. Now you notice the bright beam of a light spreading across the waves. As the sun sets, the light becomes brighter and stronger. As you continue to walk, you notice a tall lighthouse in the distance; it stands close to shore and you walk toward the lighthouse. As you approach it, you notice its strong structure. It is old, yet made to withstand the weather and sea.

• You decide to enter the lighthouse. Once inside, you climb the circular stairs . . . you grasp the railing and step by step, you go higher and higher. You feel safe as you ascend these stairs. You are going higher and higher, and now you come to the top floor of the lighthouse. There is a comfortable chair in the room at the top of the lighthouse. It looks out across the sea. You take a seat and sink into the overstuffed cushions. You watch the light beam from the lighthouse spread out over the sea. A wind has picked up over the ocean, and there seems to be a distant storm making its way to shore, tossing the waves tumultuously over one another. The light from the lighthouse calls out to the turbulent seas.

• You feel the darkness of the storm coming closer and closer. This storm holds the potency of emotion; there may be fear, frustration, or jealousy within the winds and clouds of the storm. The beam of the light invites these feelings closer. It calls out to them and beckons them to come closer. There might be feelings and emotions within you that surface as they are drawn toward the light. The feelings and emotions intensify; you can feel their force and you can feel the sharpness of these feelings. Yet they cannot harm or hurt you.

• Without resisting, notice how these intense feelings dissolve into the light cast by the lighthouse. The light envelops the emotions. The feelings—such as anger, pain, jealousy, and frustration—all soften as they enter the bright light. The light from the lighthouse becomes stronger and brighter as these feelings merge into it. After these feelings enter the light, they then emerge as clear, vibrant, positive energy. The negativity that these

emotions contained is now transformed into translucent, radiant waves.

- You may feel these feelings as they pass into the light.
  The light is strong, and it calls out into the storm.
  Meanness, anger, anxiety, stress—these, too, come
  close as the light invites them, transforms them into
  pure energy.

- You are energized and strengthened as you witness
  the process of the cleansing light. More emotions may
  surface. The light absorbs all of the wide range of emotions. You feel clear and calm. Now you notice the
  waves diminishing as the storm loses its force. Soon the
  sea is calm and serene as it spreads out before you like
  clear translucent glass underneath the moon shining in
  the night sky. It, too, spreads light, serenity, calm, and
  peace. You feel the silence all around you. You settle into
  a deep inner peace. It is in this calmness that you ask for
  guidance, which you can receive with clarity. Sit quietly
  and ask any questions that you might have. Breathe and
  receive images, information, and feelings. Just listen
  and accept whatever it is that you receive.

- Breathing calmly, take all the time you need. When
  you are ready, descend the stairway of the lighthouse.
  You are now back on the warm, sandy beach. You are
  completely in your body and you can feel movement
  in your hands and feet. You are feeling better than you
  have in a long time. Now you are nearly back in the

here and now. Count: one . . . coming back; two . . . completely in this room; three . . . open your eyes.

Affirmation: I let go, and let God. God has a plan for each of us. I am Love. I am compassionate and wise.

Mental Intuitive: Bubble of Love

Mental intuitives often have difficulties in quieting the mind. They can sometimes feel as if their thoughts never cease. They might continuously go over and over the same thought or idea, often feeling at a loss as to how to disentangle from them. Mental intuitives are at their best when they are open to receiving vibrations from the higher, transcendental mind. This will be more possible as the mental intuitive comes into balance by shifting their energy from the mind into the heart.

Too much focus in the mind creates a closed circuit that is unable to receive the inflow of energy from more elevated sources. Mental energy infused with the energy of the heart will help the mental intuitive to open to higher levels of awareness.

- Put yourself in a comfortable position that you can stay in for a long period of time. Close your eyes and take a long, deep breath. Send the energy of your breath to any part of your body that is sore, tense, or tight. Breathe in again and then exhale any stress or tension anywhere in your body. Breathe in again and let go of any thoughts, worries, or concerns of the day; let go of any stress and tension. Breathe and relax, going deeper and deeper into relaxation. Settle into the natural rhythm of your breath, relaxing and going deeper and deeper.

- Imagine a place in nature: perhaps somewhere you have been before, or you can create it right now—a warm and inviting place. Perhaps you hear the sound of water and in the background a distant stream or waterfall, soothing and relaxing. You can see trees and grass swaying in a gentle breeze. There are wildflowers of all shapes and colors playing in the sunshine. The sweet smell of grass of a deep forest is now permeating your senses, helping you to relax even deeper. The sun is shining down on you—its rays spreading warmth, love, serenity, security, and deep relaxation all through you.

- Take another deep breath and draw your awareness to the top of your head. Keep breathing and relaxing. Above your head you sense a well of pure white light. Inhale this light; it is warm and relaxing. You exhale this light, and as you do so it begins to form a bubble. The bubble of light begins to surround you. As you continue to breathe in this white light and then exhale it, the bubble becomes stronger. It protects you and allows only what is in your highest good to enter. At the same time, any stress, concern, or tension you may have is released and dissolved through the walls of the bubble.

- This space that you have created is safe. You can open your heart and allow love to flow through you. Love intensifies within the light, and it helps you to relax more and more. Relax into this light. You feel as if you can relax and soften into the bubble of white light. You are feeling lighter. You feel as if you are expanding to fill this bubble. You can go beyond your physical body, fill the bubble with your essence and spirit, and then expand beyond the bubble, gliding into open space. You feel light, lucid, and free; you *are* light. Imagine the light that you are as you now expand into brighter light and into love. You can connect with whomever or whatever you desire to merge with. You can touch anyone else's light. You can be in the presence of anyone you desire to be with. They can feel your love and your light, and you can feel theirs. This light is love and it is peace. You can reach to the skies and beyond. There are no barriers or boundaries. Expand and feel the peace that surrounds you—the love, the connection, the oneness that is you. All that you desire is instantly with you.

• Breathing in the love that encases you, allow your spirit, your wise inner self, to emerge. It may be formless, without shape or color, yet you can feel the presence of wisdom that emerges. You enter the void. Breathe. Connect to the center, the Source of all that is. You have the power to create from the source of wisdom that resides within you. Visualize your highest good unfolding in your life. You are creating all that you desire.

- You accept the wise and loving being that resides within you. You allow that being to emerge. You open yourself to the boundlessness of all knowledge and wisdom. Your consciousness expands and encompasses the realm of all-knowing. You do this lovingly, receiving and integrating your heart and your mind. They merge as one—the intelligence of love, the intelligence of the universe resounds within you. They merge and integrate. Breathe into your heart the vision of your highest good. Breathe it into your physical body. You can now receive the thoughts of the universe, of the Divine Mind. Any questions can be asked and you can receive immediate impressions, ideas, and truths. Bring them into the mind, the heart, the spirit. Stay in this state for as long as possible, relaxing and receiving.

- Now, begin coming back into the here and now. You feel yourself back in the body as your consciousness returns to its normal state. You are feeling movement in your hands and feet. You are coming into normal consciousness, feeling better than you have in a long time. When you're ready, open your eyes.

Affirmation: I am one with the Divine Mind. My thoughts are the thoughts of God. God's love flows through me.

Physical Intuitive: Body of Light

Physical intuitives often absorb into their bodies the energy of their environment. This could be the atmosphere of a stressful office or a tense family situation. They also intuit through the third chakra, the solar plexus, and hold their psychic impressions within the physical body. This can lead to poor health, exhaustion, and weight gain. Physical intuitives can come into balance by becoming aware of their natural tendency to take energy into the body; they can then learn how to release and express it. If you are a physical intuitive, this meditation will help you to become aware of and to clear your body of energetic heaviness.

- Lie or sit in a comfortable position that you can stay in for a long period of time. Close your eyes, take a long deep breath, and send the energy of your breath to any part of your body that is sore, tense, or tight. Breathe in again, and breathe out any stress or tension anywhere in your body. Breathe in again and let go of any thoughts, worries, or concerns of the day; release stress and tension. Settle into the natural rhythm of your breath and keep relaxing and going deeper and deeper.

- Imagine a place in nature—perhaps somewhere you have been before or a place you create right now. This is a warm and inviting place, and perhaps you hear the sound of water in the background. Possibly there is a distant stream or a waterfall. This place is soothing and relaxing; you can see trees and grass swaying in the gentle breeze. There are wildflowers of all shapes and colors playing in the sunshine and the sweet smell of grass of a deep forest permeates your senses. Allow yourself to relax in this environment. The sun is shining down on you; its rays are spreading warmth, love, serenity, security, and deep relaxation throughout your body.

- Imagine a warm breeze, perhaps smelling of sweet grass or flowers, lightly touching your skin. The warmth of this breeze feels safe and comforting. The breeze begins to form a bubble of warmth that surrounds you. As you take another deep breath, you can feel the walls of this bubble grow stronger and more protective of you, allowing only what is in your highest good to enter. Take another deep breath, and then draw your awareness to the top of your head. Keep breathing and relaxing, and draw your awareness to the space above your head where you might feel it quiver and tingle. You may experience the feeling of opening as your spirit expands. You are feeling relaxed, expanded, and free. Starting at the top of your head, draw your awareness all the way through your body.

  Become aware of any part of your body that may be tight or tense. There may be more than one place in your body where there is tension or tightness. Take note of where these places are. Allow your attention to go to the place in your body where you feel the most stress or tightness. Then, using your imagination, ask yourself if this place were a color, what color would it be? If this color had a texture, what would that be like? Now, allow an image to emerge that represents this energy. This can be any image at all—it might be a person, an object, a place. You may feel this image, or perhaps catch a glimpse of it, or just know it. However this image comes to you is fine. You do not have to force this. Just allow it to happen.

- Now, imagine that this image can speak to you. Imagine that it can communicate and that it has a voice. It has a message for you. Listen to it and receive your message. You can ask questions of this image. The image may change.

- Stay with it for as long as you can and receive whatever it has to offer you. When you feel that you have received as much as you can at this time, allow this energy to be absorbed into the bubble of light that surrounds you. Send the energy of this image, the tightness or the stress, to the light. Allow the place where it has been to be filled with light, white light, purifying and filling you with love and with warmth. You can continue this process in any part of your body where there is tension and tightness. All you need to do is identify the area, allow the energy to speak to you, release it to the light, and then fill the place where this energy has been with white, healing light.

- When you are ready, begin to return to the here and now, feeling refreshed and relaxed. You're feeling better than you have in a long time. You will remember everything that you have just experienced. When you are ready, you can open your eyes.

Affirmation: My body is a spiritual instrument. The divine flows through me. I am spirit in the physical. I absorb only positive energy that is in my highest good. I understand and put words to energy.

Spiritual Intuitive: The Enlightened Body

The following meditation will help the spiritual intuitive to ground spiritual energy and bring it through the body. Spiritual intuitives' biggest challenge may be to stay in the physical. Their consciousness often drifts into astral and ethereal states. They can with practice integrate their natural multidimensional perception into their conscious awareness. This meditation integrates the spirit into the physical body.

- Lie or sit in a comfortable position that you can stay in for a long period of time. Close your eyes, take a long deep breath, and send the energy of your breath to any part of your body that is sore, tense, or tight. Breathe in again. Breathe out any stress or tension anywhere in your body. Breathe in again and let go of any thoughts, worries, or concerns of the day and release the stress and tension. Go deeper and deeper into relaxation. Settle into the natural rhythm of your breath, relaxing and going deeper and deeper.

- Imagine a warm, inviting white light gathering above your head. As this light gathers and strengthens above your head, keep breathing and releasing any stress anywhere in your body. Imagine this light gently descending and caressing the top of your head.

Breathe this light in, feeling it expanding and spreading warmth and love, clearing and opening your sixth chakra, which is the center of your head. As this light descends down and through your head, it releases any toxins or heaviness and negativity. It is then lifted out through the top of your head. As the light continues to descend into your jaw and neck, let it release and relax you. It gently and warmly descends down into your shoulders, your arms, and your elbows.

- Feel the light entering your heart. Feel your heart chakra expanding. Let go of any disappointment, sadness, or grief that you might feel. Then allow your heart to fill with love. Feel this light as serenity and warmth. Feel the light spreading now to your solar plexus. You are feeling empowered by the vibration of light. You can feel self-doubt and fear being released. Now the light is traveling to the organs of your body, clearing toxins out, caressing the organs, and spreading into your second chakra. Seeds of hope are sprouting. Buds of manifestation and abundance are being nurtured by the light. The light is flowing through your hips. It is strengthening the muscles, bones, tissues, and fiber. The light reaches your first chakra.

- The light expands, and you feel a thick, multistrand web of light grounding you to the earth. Your purpose here on earth is taking root, being nurtured from above. You are vibrant and free to love, to give and to receive, and just to be. Your spirit is filled with light that reaches from the heavens to the earth. Your spirit is rooted and filled with light. Your spirit extends into the physical. The earth has a message for you; it may be a feeling, a thought. It is calling you to make your home here. It is reminding you of the beauty and joy that is the physical. You feel an orb of light surrounding you and connecting you to the earth. Feel yourself caressed in this cocoon of love and breathe it in. You allow the accumulation of toxins above your head to be scooped up by a net of light, and then it is taken into the cleansing stream of divine love. You are feeling vibrant and alive. You continue to breathe in through the top of your head, and you imagine this light descends deep into the root chakra and spreads throughout your entire body. With each breath, you feel your body accepting spiritual energy. Your muscles, cells, and organs absorb the positive radiance that envelops you. You are one. You are one in body, in mind, and in spirit.

- Slowly come back into the here and now. Take all the time that you need and then allow yourself to come into normal consciousness. Stay in the glow of spiritual luminosity as long as possible. You feel this energy in your entire body. You are feeling better than you have in a long time, as you come back to normal consciousness. Take a long, deep breath and slowly open your eyes.

Affirmations: I am Spirit in the physical. God is here. Each day the plan for my highest good unfolds. I live in the here and now in joy and harmony. I witness the divine in the mundane.

12

INTUITIVE EXERCISES
BY TYPE

Each intuitive type receives psychic energy through the modality that is most natural to them. Because of this, each type will excel in specific kinds of psychic exchanges. As you become aware of the way that you instinctively approach psychic energy, it will become easier to increase your innate talents.

Most mental intuitives practice mental telepathy without being aware that they are doing so. Mental telepathy is the ability to read the thoughts of another. These might be the thoughts of one person, a group, or even a soul group. Because mental intuitives are highly attuned to the vibration of mental energy, they can intuit trends, logic, patterns, and abstract ideas better than other types. Mental intuitives can also become very good at clairvoyance, the ability to see or view images and actual impressions of real-life events. Clairvoyance is a function of the sixth chakra, which is also called the *third eye*. Because the energy of a mental intuitive tends to be centered in the sixth chakra, they are most likely to acquire this skill.

Due to their openhearted approach to life, emotional intuitives can intuit the feelings and emotional energy of an environment, a group, or an individual. This is emotional telepathy, the ability to intuit what another may be feeling or experiencing without conscious awareness. Emotional intuitives can home in on pain or bliss, or any emotion in between, and then follow the emotional energy to its source. Like a bloodhound following a scent, the emotional intuitive can tell where, when, and how an injury occurred or pain began. They can then be adept at knowing what will heal and bring wholeness to another. When well-developed, the emotional intuitive has the ability to heal and transform the pain and emotional wounds of others. They may also have a kind of emotional clairvoyance, which is the ability to see or have impressions of others who are undergoing an emotional experience, trauma, or bliss.

Communing with the nonphysical is natural for the spiritual intuitive, which often means dreaming, visioning, imagining, and communicating with various life forms. A spiritual intuitive's psychic skill is more elusive than the other types, and they are the most likely to communicate with people who have passed over to the other side. They may sense, hear, or see deceased people, ghosts, ETs, and other nonphysical beings. Spiritual intuitives might also receive visions and messages from guides and angels more easily than the other types, and they often have a rich dream life. They may be able to channel extraordinary works of art, music, prose, and poetry.

Physical intuitives are often attuned to the energies of physical objects and the earth itself. They can thus communicate with the spirits residing in stones, crystals, plants, and animals, and they tend to do well with psychometry, the ability to read the energy information from objects. They are more concrete than the other types and will be able to psychically intuit literal messages rather than messages that are more imaginative and figurative. They seldom use symbols to interpret what they receive; instead, they tend to be straightforward and exacting. Because of these skills, they can become skilled psychic detectives who can home in on specific details and material facts. As they progress into the higher levels of psychic aptitude, physical intuitives can become powerful shamans and healers. When highly evolved, they can move, change, or alter physical matter, including the physical body. They can be capable of amazing healings.

Increasing Psychic Skills

Because most people are a combination of intuitive types, the following exercises can be practiced by everyone. It is important to work with modalities that are not your own. To strengthen your psychic capabilities, it is necessary to be open to all ways of receiving and interpreting energy. As your intuition develops, you will find that you can draw on different aspects of yourself, depending on the needs of the situation.

Try to keep an open mind while you work with these exercises. A sense of humor—and the willingness to be open to whatever your experience may be—will get you further than self-judgment and expectations that are too high. When we are beginning to develop our of intuitive powers, it can be just as helpful to be inaccurate as to be accurate; either way, we get a sense of when our psychic awareness is on target and when it is not.

Spiritual Intuitive Exercise: Enlightened Drawing

Spiritual intuitives have a natural connection to the nonphysical. Because of this, they are attuned to and can sense changes in vibration, which helps them to see auras or lights and ethereal colors. They may also have a sensitivity to sound, especially the higher frequencies, and they are more comfortable than the other types with essence and ambiguity. They can easily immerse themselves in pure energy.

This exercise appeals to the spiritual intuitive's ability to interpret and create meaning of the formless. While this is a group exercise, it can also be done with a partner. It requires drawing paper or a note pad, and pastels, colored pencils, or crayons.

Before you begin this exercise, spread out the drawing materials in front of you. This exercise starts with a simple relaxation meditation.

- Lie or sit in a comfortable position. Close your eyes, take a long deep breath, and send the energy of your breath to any part of your body that is sore, tense, or tight. Breathe in again, and then breathe out any stress or tension you find anywhere in your body. Breathe in again and breathe out, letting go of any thoughts, worries, or concerns of the day, exhaling stress and tension, breathing and relaxing, going deeper and deeper into relaxation.

- Take a few silent minutes to gently bring your awareness into your body. Then without speaking, pick drawing materials that attract your attention. Draw shapes, lines, and forms. This is stream of consciousness drawing. Do not judge what you draw. The key is just to draw. Try to stay in the energy and not to think about what you are drawing. When you feel you are finished, set your picture in the center of the group.

When everyone is finished, each person quietly selects someone else's picture. One by one, each person tells a story about the picture they selected. The story can be fantasy, make-believe, whatever comes spontaneously. This exercise is often fun, yielding surprising insight and psychic information.

In a recent class, Barbara made a simple drawing of a fish with large eyes looking through the surface of the water. Jeff picked up Barbara's drawing and talked about how this fish felt different from the other fish. He said that it did not feel part of the larger school of fish. It was alone, searching for something, though it was not sure for what. Jeff said that the fish had not honored its own special gifts enough. Jeff said that instead of searching for its reflection outside of the water, it only had to look within to see its own beauty.

This short interpretation left Barbara close to tears. She identified with what Jeff saw in her picture. She had been struggling with the issues he mentioned.

Mental Intuitive: Synchronicity

Mental intuitives enjoy investigating and learning and do well with complexity and multilevel thinking. Astrology, numerology, and the I Ching are a few of the systems whose methods they can use to understand and organize the world around them. An exercise that a mental intuitive does well with uses synchronicity. It allows the mind to think, but it takes the thought to higher levels of awareness.

It is necessary to do this exercise with a number of books close by. Begin this exercise by writing down a concern or question. You may have more than one pressing issue; if this is so, write them all down and then select the one question or concern that seems the most important.

- Close your eyes and meditate on this question. Let any stress, fear, concern, expectation, or excitement you have about the question surface. Take a few long, deep breaths and release any stress you have as you exhale. Continue breathing and releasing, focusing on the breath. As you breathe, imagine a protective white light enveloping you. This light begins to form a bubble that completely surrounds you and allows only what is in your highest good to enter your aura or come close to you. As you sit within this bubble of protective light, you can ask your guides, your Higher Self, or the divine to assist you. Ask for guidance, for the highest good to be revealed to you. Imagine you are releasing this concern to the highest good. Try to detach from the outcome and ask to be led or guided.

- When you feel that you have, as much as possible, released the question to a Higher Power, open your eyes. You are surrounded by books. Pick up the book that you feel most drawn to and open it at random. Allow your eyes to be drawn to a certain page, to a particular paragraph or passage. Read the paragraph or sentence. At this point, it is normal to want to do it again, as rarely does the paragraph or passage make sense at the first reading. *Do not pick another book, or another page or passage.* Instead, sit quietly, close your eyes, and ask your guides to help you to understand what you've just read.

- You will most likely be tempted to try and interpret the passage with your logic-driven consciousness. Try to resist this temptation.

- Now breathe, go back into meditation, and listen for your guidance. Mental intuitives can open their mind and experience higher influences. Try to remain open to the experience, without expecting guidance to come in any particular form. Often the guidance that we receive comes in the form of feelings such as comfort, love, and safety. Guidance may come to you as a memory, perhaps an event during which you learned something about yourself or life. You might also receive thoughts, or a block of knowing.

- There is a feeling, a moment of transcendence that often happens with this exercise. When you are in this higher state of awareness, you may feel expanded or in a dreamlike state of creative knowing. Write down your thoughts, feelings, and whatever else comes to you, even if it does not make sense or seems irrelevant. As you return to normal consciousness, what seemed obvious or conspicuous will fade away, and you may not fully understand the message for a few days or even weeks.

Emotional Intuitive: Partner Meditation

Emotional intuitives work well with partners, and are often more motivated and work harder when they feel they are being of service to another. This exercise focuses on the connection between the emotions and the physical body. Emotional intuitives can often access powerful currents of Universal Life Force through their desire to love and care for others. Love is powerful, and intuition works best when it is fueled by love. When we allow love to flow through us, our potential is unlimited.

- Sit comfortably, facing your partner. Breathe into your heart and allow it to open. Close your eyes, take a long deep breath, and send the energy of your breath to any part of your body that is sore, tense, or tight.

Breathe in again, then breathe out any stress or tension you find anywhere in your body. Settle into the natural rhythm of your breath. Imagine you can draw breath from above your head. Your head may tingle as you imagine your seventh chakra opening like a joyful flower accepting the sun. You draw down through the head this vibrant, white-light energy. You feel energized as you draw this breath into the heart and then exhale through the heart. Continue to breathe from the top of the head and exhale through the heart. As you exhale, you feel your heart open, releasing rich waves of love.

- This breath begins to form a white-light bubble surrounding you and your partner. With each breath the wall of this bubble grows stronger and more capable of amplifying the psychic energy that you and your partner are generating. The bubble allows only what is in your highest good to enter, to come close to the two of you. You and your partner are safe, protected. Breathing and relaxing within this psychic bubble, draw your awareness to your heart. Feel your breath flowing through your heart, the lightness of this breath and the feelings of warmth and caring that accompany it. Send the warmth of this love, this light, through your heart and to your partner. Send unconditional love. Feel how good it is to love unconditionally, without expectation, free and easy.

- Allow this love to be accepted in whatever way feels most comfortable and safe for your partner. At the same time, accept the love flowing to you. It is a gift to give love unconditionally and it is a gift to receive. This love, the richness and depth of this love, forms a bridge of energy between you and your partner. You can feel the connection between you and your partner; you feel your oneness. Send this love and these feelings of oneness to your partner. Send your awareness to your partner. Starting at the top of your partner's head, begin to scan his or her body. As you slowly scan your partner's body, become aware of what part of the body your attention feels drawn to. You can then ask questions of whatever area of your partner's body you are attending to.

- What feelings or emotions are coming forward from this area? Try to put a name to the feeling, the emotion that you are connecting to. Listen calmly. Perhaps you sense a color or shades of a color. If this energy were a color, which color would it be? Continue to be open and receptive, listening for any ache, any tension or pain. Continue to scan your partner's body from the top of the head down to the feet. Pause. Take your time. Listen. Let your awareness be drawn to wherever you are led. You may see images; they may be literal or figurative. Thoughts or memories may surface, revealing clues and information that don't seem to make sense. Just let whatever needs to flow in, flow in. You can make notes of what it is you become aware of.

- Imagine yourself as a conduit for loving and healing energy to flow from you to your partner. Send it to the part of your partner's body where you have sensed any pain, aches, or burdens. Allow your heart to expand even further, continuing to send love to wherever you sense it is needed. Powerful waves of love are flowing through you, healing and at the same time allowing yourself to be healed, to be known and cared for. The healer and the healed are one. The bond of divine love is flowing between you, creating harmony.

- Be open to any message that comes to you. When you're ready, begin to allow the bubble to soften. As you return fully and completely into your body, the bubble is dispersing. When you return to normal consciousness, you will remember everything you just experienced in perfect clarity. You will feel better than you have in a long time. Open your eyes now.

This exercise can reveal all kinds of information. It is not unusual to become aware of your partner's difficult memories or deep-seated pain. If this happens, ask your guides to help you to lovingly express this to your partner. It is important that we respect the privacy of others. Even when our intent is to be a conduit of healing, we need to be mindful of how delicate and fragile we can be when we are in this open and receptive intuitive state.

This exercise can also be done with another through proxy. It is not necessary for the other person to be physically present. You can invite the presence of anyone into this healing white-light bubble with you. This is a helpful exercise to use when those we love are going through difficult times or illness. It is important to ask their permission to do this special prayer and meditation for them.

Physical Intuitive: Psychometry

Psychometry is the ability to intuit the vibration of a physical object and then interpret the energy into useful information. Physical intuitives naturally connect with the energy of physical objects. While this exercise is best done in a group, it can also be done individually.

- In a group setting, each person puts a ring, earring, watch, necklace, or other personal item into a bowl or bag. The bowl is then passed around the circle, and each person randomly takes out an item. When everyone is holding an object, they sit quietly with eyes closed. While in this receptive state, the participants become aware of any feelings, thoughts, images, smells, or sensations that occur.

- Do not dismiss anything as unimportant! People practicing psychometry for the first time often feel as if they're making things up. I have had people report all kinds of experiences during this exercise.

In one group, a woman reported that she smelled fried chicken as she held someone's ring; it was later revealed that the ring she was holding belonged to a sixteen-year-old girl who loved fried chicken and said she had been thinking of stopping at a fast-food restaurant after class to get some. In another class, a woman seemed reluctant to talk about what her impressions were of the ring she held. When she did share, she cautiously talked about a feeling of chaos, gray storm clouds, and depression. The woman whose ring it was told us that it was actually her grandmother's ring. Her grandmother had recently died, and during the last several years of her life the grandmother had suffered from severe dementia and lived in a nursing home. The ring still carried her vibration.

You can also do this exercise by holding your mail in your hand and "read" it before you open it. Another variation is to pick up stones, feathers, shells, or other natural objects and see what impressions you receive.

Physical intuitives are also naturally adept at communicating with animals. With a pet or other animal, open your mind and listen to images, thoughts, or feelings that come to you from the animal. It is helpful to ask questions to get the energy circulating, and it is important to clear the mind before you begin. Be honest about what your expectations are and what you would like to hear.

One of the most difficult aspects of doing this psychometry exercise alone is being able to discern what you would like to receive and what the energy is truly emitting. For this reason, group work is the preferred method.

Specific Questions

Our desire to "know" and to "intuit" information and guidance is usually strongest when we are in situations and circumstances that personally affect us. Unfortunately, it can be difficult to clearly read energy when we desire a certain outcome. To be able to perceive conditions accurately, we have to be somewhat detached, since our emotions, thoughts, and beliefs can influence our perceptions. We can sometimes read our own fears or anxieties instead of the true conditions. Or we can be sure that we will get exactly what we want and not put effort into creating the desired end result. Instead of focusing our attention only on reading the probable energetic outcomes of future events, it may at times be more helpful to direct the flow of psychic energy in a more productive and positive direction.

Intuition not only provides insight into and information about the circumstances and events we find ourselves in, it can also provide a boost of high-vibration energy to fuel the manifestation of positive outcomes. Remember that psychic energy is energy. It is not bound to time or space. It is not constrained by the material world. It is possible to focus our intuitive-psychic power to create what we desire. Psychic energy correctly applied can increase and amplify the flow of energy for our highest good.

The following exercise can be used in almost any circumstance that we find ourselves in, whether we have relationship issues or health-related and financial concerns. Although this exercise addresses the particular strengths of each intuitive type, everyone can benefit by practicing all of the variations.

Directing the Flow

- The first stage of this exercise is active listening and observing. This is the more receptive intuitive state that we achieve through relaxing, breathing, and focusing our attention on the quiet place within. After relaxing and deep centered breathing, allow an image to emerge of the event about which you are concerned. For instance, perhaps you have a job interview, and you want to know how it will go. Or maybe you want to know if the job you're applying for is right for you. Imagine as clearly as possible the interview. Create a picture of it in your imagination. Try to add as many details as possible to the image, such as the environment of the interview and what you are wearing. Make sure to include the interviewer! Try not to become stressed out if you are not seeing the image clearly or if it changes. Just relax and do the best you can do. You can just make it up and let it be, whatever it is. There is no right or wrong way to do this.

- With a detached attitude, almost as if you are observing the scene as a reporter would, ask yourself the following types of questions:

For the emotional intuitive: When I view this scene, how do I feel? Am I elated, disappointed, hopeless, excited, or happy?

For the mental intuitive: Draw attention to your thoughts and beliefs. When I view the scene, do I have a sense of accomplishment? Can I grow and learn in this job? Can I contribute to this work environment? Do I have enough confidence to get and keep this job?

For the physical intuitive: When I view the scene, what sensations do I feel in my body? Is my stomach churning? Is my body tight, throat tense, or jaw rigid? When I project myself in this job, do I feel alive with energy flowing through me?

For the spiritual intuitive: When I view the scene, am I present and do I feel connected to it? Do I feel bored and bland? Am I able to focus or does my attention drift away? Does the image feel vibrant or distant?

- The second part of the exercise involves sending vital positive energy to the image. Again imagine the scene, the job interview, but instead of being an observer, this time you will be an active participant. Take a deep breath, imagining you are breathing in clear, vibrant, loving, white-light energy. Then add energy through focusing and projecting to the scene.

The emotional intuitive will send love, positive energy through the heart. Feel love flow through you; imagine the scene infused with love. Love is creating your highest good.

The mental intuitive will send positive thoughts. Lift the energy into the mind. Expand your energy into the sixth chakra, the third eye. See yourself successful, knowing that you draw to yourself the perfect job. Affirm your belief that your highest good is manifesting.

If you are a physical intuitive, you will feel positive power flowing through you. Send energy into the solar plexus, the third chakra, and feel the power to create your highest good.

Feel your body open and express positive influence. Feel the power to create all that you desire and allow it to flow through you.

If you are a spiritual intuitive, you will feel energy flowing through you from the seventh chakra, infusing all of your aspirations with joy. Imagine light energy flowing through you and connecting you to right action. It flows in the direction of your highest good. You are Spirit in action. Feel your spirit lift into abundance and your body vibrate with success.

Releasing Outcomes

- After you have focused your energy in this active and creative way, calmly sit, listen, and be open to any impressions, feelings, or thoughts that emerge. Be open to whatever surfaces, even if it does not seem particularly helpful. Your intuition may come to you as a feeling of comfort. You may see an image or hear a message, or you may have a thought, a revelation about yourself in this job. As much as possible, release any need to control the outcome. Often it is a blessing not to receive what we desire. A better job may be coming your way. Your highest good may materialize in a form that at the moment you cannot recognize. Affirm that your highest good is on its way.

This exercise can also be done in a group or with a partner. We often are more willing to help others than we are to empower ourselves. You can repeat this exercise as often as you would like. Each time you do it, begin by observing your initial reaction to the scene, empower it with energy directed to your highest good, and then quietly listen to any impressions that may surface.

When we supply a positive flow of energy to our circumstances, the changes can be surprising. Energy responds to our intent. Most predictions are based on the probable flow of energy. We have the power to shape, mold, and affect what happens in our lives. Our free will dictates that we can strengthen or deter the good that comes to us.

13

SPIRIT
GUIDES

~~~~~~~~~~~~~~~~~~~~~~~~~~~~~~~~~~~~~~~

Most people seek out spiritual help only after they have exhausted all other possible sources. It takes trust and faith to release our troubles and worries to the care of the unseen. Psychic awareness is a form of intelligence, and some people have a higher degree of spiritual aptitude than others. This aptitude lies along the continuum of diverse intelligences—we can be highly kinesthetic, musical, artistic, analytical, or intuitive. As our spiritual maturity evolves, it becomes easier for us to listen to and act on our intuition.

We begin to recognize the complexity of life and the variety of expressions that life can take. As we do this, we will rely less on the material and physical, and more on the subtle and spiritual.

Although it can be hard to imagine that we have in our midst loving and wise energies that care for us, most people are comforted when I talk to them about their spirit guides, angels, and teachers. These guides serve as a mirror of our own evolved Higher Self, which is the soul within each one of us that is eternal, loving, and wise. Our guides are aspects of our multidimensional self. Our guides and angels form a bridge extending over time, space, and form, reaching out to us from the divine. They are perfected facets of the cosmic web where we are all interconnected. As we become more aware of our guides, angels, and other spiritual helpers, we wake up to our own divine nature. As sap is drawn out of the tree, our spirit helpers call forth our rich inner core.

Our guides and angels sometimes know us more intimately than those who are close to us in the physical. It can be difficult for some of us to accept that we can be known and loved despite our faults and flaws, and it is surprising that something so divine in nature would choose to hang out with us and share our space. Even though it can be hard to imagine how they can find any interest in our day-to-day affairs, their care and concern for us can be astounding. It might seem beyond our comprehension to be so selfless, but they know us, feel us, and love us.

Most of us want to know who they are, what their names are, how to contact them. I have found, however, that some guides are not comfortable being called by name. They tell me that there is too much separation in a name. Higher guides would rather encourage us to think in terms of oneness. As we journey closer to our ultimate connection with God, they say, we lose our sense of operating as separate beings.

Just as snowflakes are uniquely different in design from one another yet their substance is the same, so it is with our guides, who are on the path to perfection. They have advanced beyond our realm. They no longer need to have the experience of Earth life in order to grow; it is through love and devotion that they draw close to us. They also have lessons to learn through their work with us. Just as we attend classes and workshops and read books to learn about ourselves and the world around us, so do our guides teach us about the realm of spirit. They do not want us to idolize them; instead, their desire is to tell us that we are all one. Who better would be able to instruct us than those who make their home in the spiritual realms?

Many guides are learning how to operate from a soul group instead of from an individualized perceptive. Much of the energy we would term "spirit guide" is, therefore, actually not a single soul as we might define it. As energy purifies, it becomes less defined by boundaries and separation. When we work with these guides, we are learning to connect to potent energy that may use us as channels for a soul group to express unique ideas here on Earth.

Spirit often chooses us to work on projects and undertakings that can influence others on a large scale. Spirit does this by igniting in us a passion to serve others in some way. This might be a cause or a desire to teach and uplift others. Peter and Sheila belong to a community of people who are devoted to planetary healing. They gather together on a monthly basis to pray and channel love and healing to areas in the world where suffering or devastation have taken place. In the past few years through ritual and ceremony, they have attempted to contact and work in unison with the Devic kingdom and nature spirits to ease the effects of global warming. They endeavor to open channels for the calm release of the toxins and negativity that threaten the balance and harmony of the planet. They sent waves of peaceful energy to Asia after the tsunami in 2004, and to New Orleans after Hurricane Katrina. They have also focused their attention on California, where earthquakes are predicted, in an attempt to nullify the quakes.

We often cannot fully comprehend how important we may be to Spirit. We are never required to sacrifice ourselves or our soul identity by our guides and angels. We are accepted and honored by Spirit as unique expressions of God.

Spirit Comedians

When I begin a reading for someone, it is not unusual for me to start laughing as I connect with their guides. Guides can be incredibly funny. Years ago, struggling in therapy through some of the painful experiences of my childhood, I had intense feelings of pain and grief. During that time, when resting or meditating, I would often see one of my guides, a Native American man, doing all kinds of crazy stunts on a spirit horse. He would be riding as fast as he could, only to then stumble off a cliff and fall through the sky, making all kinds of silly gestures and facial expressions.

At first I thought maybe there was some deeper meaning to his antics. I watched closely. He never gave up until I started to laugh. Sometimes it felt as though he was coming very close to me, as if he wanted me to feel his silliness even more intensely. In some of my down moments, he would appear, ridiculously dressed, doing any silly stunt he could to get my attention. I am grateful now for his intervention. At the time, I did not really understand it, but now, after so many readings and work with others who are suffering, I understand the gift that humor offers us. There is openness and a lightness that laughter creates.

My guides have never seemed to offer me much pity in difficult times. Another time when I was working on some challenging issues and experiencing difficult emotions, I reached out to my guides for their support. I was looking for comfort, and their lack of sympathy surprised me. Then I received the message from them that my suffering was my choice. I could move on or stay mired in my sadness. This was not the response I expected. I wanted support and empathy. What I received surprised me enough to jar me out of my miserable state. I was shocked by what felt then like insensitivity; over time, I have learned some of the differences between divine love and our human interpretations of what we expect love to be.

Nor are my guides overly concerned with my version of reality. They want to uplift me to see beyond the human condition. They sometimes laugh at me with big, huge laughs. They think it is so funny that I think that I am "Sherrie Dillard." They know me as a soul, as a spirit; their knowing helps me to know myself in this way.

It is usually difficult to translate a joke from a guide or a loved one in spirit. The humor of Spirit goes beyond words. For example, I had a client who was very serious about her work. She felt called to be a healer and was searching out different paths, from acupuncture to the ministry. She was very active and busy in the world. When I started to do a reading for her, a short, stocky, rough-looking male guide made himself known to me. He found it amusing that she was trying to find a path, when surrounding her was a brilliant spiritual light. He kept tapping her on the shoulder, trying to point out the freedom and love all around her. He thought it hilarious that she kept her nose to the ground, that she was focused on the dull and confusing, and he said that she spent more time and energy keeping her blinders on than just letting herself feel the Light that was her.

It was a bit difficult for me to express all of this to her. I tried, but she still felt she needed a certain path to follow. She felt that she had to "find herself." She felt that it would be unpractical and lazy to just accept and feel the Light. Feeling the Light, she told me, would not pay her bills or work out well with her husband. She just didn't understand the transformative power that the Light would have on her. She couldn't accept that opening her consciousness would open to her a path of manifestation.

Guides often frustrate us into change. We do not always get the kind of advice we are seeking. When we want comfort, what they often give us is practical advice. When we want to know how to make some money, they laugh and poke fun at us. Simply put, their agenda is not our agenda. Even more importantly, we cannot control and manipulate them. Our pleas of desperation when we want things to happen in a certain way probably will not work on them. Honesty and sincerity make more of an impression than pleading and whining. They love it when we work hard at gaining their favor. They love it when we take a chance. When we leap with faith and count on love to embrace and support us, when we make a courageous stand, that's when they applaud and draw closer.

Our desire for their help is often put to the test. Are we willing to act the fool for love? Can we stand by their side and laugh at the stresses and anxieties of our world? I tell people that if they really want the help of an evolved spirit guide, they will have to give of themselves in a real way. This could be why the practice of sacrifice was popular for so many centuries. Guides do ask us to give, but they do not want us to give them our children, a goat, or money. They want us to give away our ego, our self-centered desires, and our expectations. For this they will shower us with blessings beyond our imaginings.

Communicating with Guides and Angels

As we usually perceive it in our everyday lives, the world is very small. Yet there are multitudes of life forms, many non-physical, surrounding us and sharing space with us. Guides, angels, loved ones, teachers, interested and curious spirits all inhabit the space that we call our own. Those whom we love and who love us reside within our energy field. During readings, people often ask me to pass on messages to their guides or loved ones. In almost all situations, those in spirit can hear, see, and feel us better than we can perceive them. Spirits are often able to manipulate electrical currents, lights, and television and phone lines. They do this to get our attention, to try and let us know they are with us. Often, they do this to try and comfort us.

Most people feel unsuccessful in their attempts to communicate with spirit. This is often because people have a pre-conceived idea of what such communication will be like. We expect to clearly hear words or see visions. We want to get answers in the way that suits us. But spirits are often working hard on their end to break into our physical vibration, and we miss their signals.

Developing spiritual seeing, hearing, and knowing sensitivities is essential if we are to communicate with the unseen. Our spiritual senses are more subtle than our physical senses. Spiritual seeing, for example, is highly imaginative. It may involve symbols, colors, numbers, or fragments of information from our own memories. Psychic vibrations stimulate our mind to create impressions from the energy that it is receiving.

Images such as a river, an eagle, or a diamond ring are probably not literal messages, but rather symbols our mind uses to represent information we intuit.

If we pay attention to these visions, images, and symbols that we pick up, we begin to notice that patterns are forming. Our minds organize psychic information. In time, it will get easier to recognize the meaning inherent in the invisible psychic energy flowing to us. It's like learning to play a musical instrument or speak a new language. Eventually our mind adapts and arranges psychic stimuli, helping us to understand what the message means.

Spiritual hearing tends to be softer and more refined than our physical hearing. With our spiritual ears, we may hear a word, a phrase, or a complete sentence. It may sound like a whisper, the famous still small voice. Often a word or sentence repeats itself over and over, sometimes increasing in intensity.

Intuitive information is not flat and static. It is stimulating. It may feel like a buzz of vibration, a rush of energy. We may feel this energy emotionally. Psychic energy can stimulate within us a huge range of emotions and affect us profoundly. Laughter, sadness, love, joy, and peace can all accompany a spiritual message. When we receive guidance that is too reasoned, without a flow of energy and warmth, it is probably not from spirit.

Messages from spirit often seem to be coming from our own thinking. We feel them as our own knowing, our own ideas. For most people, it takes time and practice to know whether what they are receiving is from spirit or from their own inner imaginings. But psychic energy has its own unique feel. Eventually our inner senses will become more familiar with it. It's like tuning to a radio or television station. There are various wavelengths of vibration that contain organized information. We can, with time, become adept at choosing where to focus our attention. With refined awareness it becomes easier to connect to a psychic source.

Our guides, angels, and other spiritual teachers are here to assist us. They tune into our consciousness as we attempt to tune into theirs. They are always with us, always devoted to our growth and unfoldment. For them, there is no time and space as we conceive them. Our guides are experiencing what we will one day experience. They are patient and encouraging with our attempts to know them; they are flattered and honored by our efforts. They respond to our requests for help and assistance, and they love to play and hear our laughter.

How to Engage Your Guides

Most of us are not aware of how and when our guides are nearby. Their influence usually feels like an idea that suddenly occurs to us or a thought that keeps surfacing in our minds. Because they act through our various chakras, we often interpret their energy as our own. We attract guides who are proficient and advanced in the issues, talents, and lessons we are engaged in, and guides are attracted to us for their growth as well as ours. In the spiritual realms, they experience the oneness of the universe much more strongly than we do here on Earth. As they help us to develop, they also progress and strengthen their union with God.

Giving without expectation, practicing unconditional love, and learning patience are attributes that are highly regarded in the spirit world. We can enhance our awareness of the presence of our guides by expressing love and concern for others. Selfless love increases our spiritual vibration and draws potent spiritual helpers to us. The more we show an interest in a conscious connection with our guides and angels, the more we will be given in guidance and support. To feel the connection, it is important to listen and to spend time in quiet meditation. This can feel a little crazy at first. Sitting alone and opening ourselves to unseen influences can take some getting used to. But it is important to ask for guidance that is in our own and others' highest good.

Just as we would not open the doors to our home and allow anyone to walk in, so should we only open ourselves to unseen influences that are from the Light. I always begin a meditation or reading with a simple prayer in which I ask for protection and loving guidance for the highest good of all.

The unseen worlds contain many different types of energy. As in our physical world, there are those we can trust and others we cannot trust. In the nonphysical world, there are divine loving guides and angels, but there are also lower etheric thought forms and energies that may not have the ability or desire to be helpful. There are ghosts that are stubborn, confused spirits that have remained close to the earth after their physical death. They may view us as intruders and enjoy eliciting fear and shock from us. There are mischievous earth-based elementals such as gnomes and sprites that might view us as fair game for disturbing tricks and pranks.

We are generally responsible for what we attract and the connections we make in both the physical and spiritual worlds. When we ask with an open heart and for the highest good for ourselves and others, we call to us powerful divine helpers. Our guides will always respond to our requests when we are sincere. It is best to ask for help in areas that matter most to us. The higher realms are most interested in our becoming aware of our connection to the Universal Life Force. They desire that we live as co-creators with the divine; they empower us to establish our heaven on Earth; and they cannot be seduced to fulfill our fantasies. Our egos can convince us that certain events and things will make us happy, but our guides cannot be fooled by our desires. They will not promote self-centeredness and selfishness. They long to love us and to teach us how to create a life of joy and fulfillment.

Our guides and angels do not judge our growth in terms of "success" or "failure." They seek only to be of service to our highest good. We ask our guides from our human perspective for what we want, but their answer speaks to our spirit. What we get does not always look like what we asked for.

It can be hard for us to understand the simplicity and ease of the realms of Divine Light. We can hardly understand such a noble way of being, but this is what most guides are trying to teach us. When we can create from love and not fear, we immediately become empowered. This kind of creation is bigger than we are. It boosts us up into a level of being where we know that there is endless possibility and abundance. The spiritual realms call to us to live as they do, and so our guides teach us to give with pleasure, without thought of return. They are not interested in only satisfying our human needs. They come to us to wake us to our divine nature.

We are in the presence of our guides, angels, and the divine whenever we desire to be. The more we become aware of their presence and the more we listen to and accept their guidance, the more we will trust our relationship with them. Our guides communicate to us through our emotions, our thoughts, our experiences, and the unexpected.

Sharon's adult daughter, Beth, was having difficulties with her boyfriend. She confided to Sharon often, and Sharon listened to her and gave her the best advice she could. But as Beth and her boyfriend continued to struggle, Sharon became anxious. She was worried because her daughter seldom took her advice. So Sharon asked for help from her guides and angels. She wanted to help Beth, but she did not know how. The day following her pleas of help from her guides, Sharon later told me, she was given a message over and over. She started her morning working out at the gym, where she overhead the conversation of the two people working out next to her. One was talking about her own children and how powerless she felt in helping them. Her friend calmly reminded her that her children were adults and entitled to learn through their mistakes, and suggested to the distraught woman that she let her children make their own decisions.

At lunchtime, Sharon went home and turned on the television. She caught the last part of a show on which the expert psychologist was giving the same advice Sharon had heard at the gym that morning: "Allow your grown children to make their own mistakes. Love them and give them space."

Later that same day, Sharon was flipping through a magazine in the waiting room of her dentist's office. Again, she came across the same message, this time in an advice column, and this time the message was stronger. *Butt out*, the columnist wrote to a concerned mother.

Sharon told me that she had more peace that evening than she'd had for a long time. The message—*butt out*—was not the help she thought she wanted from her guides. She wanted a plan, guidance, maybe a miracle to make her daughter happy. But she understood the wisdom of the message she received. She released the situation to her daughter's Higher Self, and let go.

Visualization Exercise:
Connecting with Your Guides

Begin by writing down a situation or problem you or a loved one may be experiencing. Then write down whatever comes to you in the way of a solution or outcome. Take your time. Come up with as many options and alternatives as you can think of. Then get quiet and practice the following meditation.

- Put yourself in a comfortable position that you can stay in for a long period of time. Close your eyes and take a long deep breath, sending the energy of your breath to any part of your body that is sore, tense, or tight. Breathe and relax, going deeper and deeper into relaxation. Settle into the natural rhythm of your breathing.

- Imagine a place in nature. Perhaps you have been there before or perhaps you are creating it right now. This place is warm and inviting. Perhaps you hear the sound of water in the background, a distant stream or waterfall. The sounds are soothing and relaxing. You can see trees and grass swaying in the breeze, wildflowers of all shapes and colors playing in the sunshine. You can smell the sweet scent of grass of a deep forest. Allow yourself to relax in this environment. The sun is shining down on you, its rays spreading warmth, love, serenity, security, and deep relaxation all through your body.

- Take another deep breath and draw your awareness to the top of your head. Imagine a sphere of pure light appearing around your head, expanding. You may feel a tingling, or see flashes of indigo, purple, or sparkling gold and white light, transparent and expanding. You feel the presence of a guide, an angel, a teacher drawing close. This is a wise and loving being who has come to assist you, to support and love you. Allow your heart to open to this presence. Feel the warm connection to this love, to this light, and love draws closer.

- You can now release any of your concerns, questions, or stress into this supportive light. Let go, fully and completely, of whatever worries you have carried with you. Let go of your concerns. Know that you are releasing them to a wise, loving source. As you let go, allow your heart to open to receive any guidance that comes to you. It may come as a feeling, an image, a thought, a knowing, a symbol, a scent, even a sound.

- Perhaps you can feel the guide drawing closer. Be open to whatever presents itself in any way that it comes to you. Trust the source that envelops you in love and peace. Stay with whatever comes to you. If the message is unclear, ask for clarity. Breathe into the energy and allow it to intensify. Be open and receptive, allowing in light, wisdom, and clarity. Spend as much time as possible in this open, receiving attitude. If your mind begins to wander, quietly bring it to center by focusing on your breath. Relax and breathe, open to what is without forcing anything to happen. When you are ready, slowly come back into normal consciousness. You will remember everything you have experienced.

- Feeling better than you have in a long time, begin to come fully and completely back into your body. When you are completely present, open your eyes. You may want to take notes immediately after the meditation. You will find that an ongoing journal will help you to keep track of persistent symbols, messages, and guidance.

Often when we practice this meditation, we might feel as if nothing significant has happened. It is not unusual to receive guidance and insight hours or days later. Perhaps while we are driving in the car or taking a walk, seemingly out of nowhere—like the breeze blowing through an open window—we sense the presence of an angel, guide, or spiritual teacher.

14

THE GUIDES WHO HELP EACH TYPE

For the most part, we draw to us guides whose soul plan is similar to our own. We may share common goals and interests with these enlightened beings who can help us navigate our way through the spiritual seas. Even when we are not aware of their presence, they are assisting us. The best way to attract a high-level guide is to seek to be of service to others and to wish to be a positive peaceful presence in the world. Guides are not interested in building up our ego or simply supplying us with answers to our questions; they seek to teach us to grow in love, understanding, and service. They want to draw us closer to God and away from self-centeredness. Our task is to ask for assistance and guidance, then open the door to their help. Without our consent, they cannot act or lead us.

We can benefit greatly from consciously working with enlightened guides and teachers. Through our work, hobbies, or other studies, these guides and teachers will lead us to whatever might assist us along our path. They will present to us the next step in our growth. Our lives can take on a creative, interesting vividness; we will live in Technicolor. Like plants living in deep soil and fed with pure water and rich sunshine, we have a direct line to the source of life and light.

The Emotional Intuitive's Guides

We succeed best in consciously connecting with our guides and angels through our natural intuitive strengths. If we are emotionally inclined, then we will be more likely to feel the presence of our guides as love and comfort. Because guides and angels ride waves of love and caring, an emotional intuitive may be able to feel the presence of a guide earlier than the other types.

Emotional intuitives are already on a path of love, already striving to live with an open heart. They are also aware of others' suffering and like to be involved in service and healing. The guides who work with emotional intuitives thus tend to have been healers and helpers in their Earth lives. Many healers on the earth plane have attracted powerful guides, who continue to be devoted to healing. They will charge an emotional intuitive's energy field with love and healing.

Emotional intuitives also work with the angelic realm. All people are, in one way or another, loved, cared for, and guided by angels, but many emotional intuitives will have angels who work in unison with them. Many of those tireless, devoted people who work in hospitals, hospices, or with abused children are connected to large assemblies of angels.

The guides and angels of an emotional intuitive may appear as soft spheres of light and warmth that cultivate the seeds of compassion and openheartedness. Many emotional intuitives have had painful or difficult childhoods, and may have from a young age been forced to live with intensified emotions. They may have needed their guides' assistance to strengthen and protect them from an early age. This makes them skilled at understanding and dealing with difficult situations and people. It is distressing, but for some people the most love and support that they have ever experienced has come from the higher unseen realms. The connection between an emotional intuitive and their guide is a bond of love and support.

Guides can help us to make our way through the sea of emotional energy. Guides who work through emotional energy are able to attune themselves to the emotional auric layer in the energy field, which is centered in our heart chakra and extends from our body. When we allow ourselves to feel our emotions, guides can transform us, transporting us from one state of being to another. Feelings that we block, repress, and do not acknowledge will create knots and obstructions in our energy field and eventually in our bodies, creating depression, anxiety, and stress. Our guides use feelings to move us to grow and change. They mirror love, forgiveness, and compassion, and they encourage and empower us through what we feel is difficult and uncomfortable.

The emotional auric level is sensitized not just to our own emotions, but to the emotions of others as well. The psychic energy that carries these emotions is highly charged and can be intense. If we believe that all that we feel and experience is our own, we can become overwhelmed and confused. Emotional energy is like a river flowing through and around us, and emotional intuitives tend to become emotional sponges, soaking up that river.

Guides help emotional intuitives transform strong feelings into heart-centered wisdom. They assist us in knowing what our emotional energy is and what we might be picking up from others and our environment in that river of energies. They help us to move through the sometimes overwhelming emotions that flow in the currents and rapids. One way they do this is by expanding our awareness of other intuitive modalities. An emotional intuitive can learn to operate from a mental, spiritual, or physical approach. Emotional intuitives can strive to understand energy by using a more mental outlook. They can question what is happening to them, which emotions are surfacing and why. Many emotional intuitives are helped by a quiet inner dialogue with their guides.

Emotional intuitives can use emotion to grow spiritually and psychically. When we are on the spiritual path, our emotions can fuel transformation. Feelings of joy and love can guide us in making decisions and choices. These emotions are the guideposts that help us to identify what is in our highest good. Being of service to others and showing forgiveness and compassion can lead us into the mansion of oneness with the divine. In the consciousness of oneness, we can begin to interpret emotion as valuable information that holds great amounts of energy that can speak to us. It has a tangible vibration, a story to tell. We can communicate with this energy by asking questions of it, then actively listening to whatever surfaces.

Katy told me she felt almost paralyzed by stress. Plagued by anxiety and fear, she could feel her chest tightening and constricting. Katy is single and in her fifties. She is the oldest of her siblings, and both her parents died about ten years ago. Katy works as an administrative assistant at a local university, a job at which she is competent but bored.

Katy told me that she had no idea why she was so anxious. Her job is secure; she was not aware of anything particular in her life that would be causing her to feel so anxious. She wanted me to connect with her guides to see if there was any looming disaster in the future that she might be anxious about. What her guides communicated to me, however, was not what Katy had asked for. What I heard from them was that Katy was subconsciously reacting to an anniversary. I told her that someone whom she had been close to, who was now in spirit, would have celebrated a birthday at this time. She started crying and told me that her mother's birthday would have been a couple of days before our session. Katy had not had a good relationship with her mother, who had passed without a sense of peace between them. Katy felt that she had not fully forgiven her mother. She wanted to, but she still felt hurt from her mother's lack of love and attention when Katy was young.

I asked Katy to close her eyes and talk to her mother. As she connected with her mother's spirit, Katy felt the warmth of her guardian angel close by; she felt supported and protected by her angelic presence. Katy asked for her mother's spirit to come close. As she did this, she felt immediately in her mother's presence. Katy told me that she received from her mother the feeling that her mother finally understood the hardship that she had put Katy through. Now able to recognize how she had made Katy feel as a child, her mother apologized for the pain that she caused Katy. Her mother said she had been overwhelmed as a young mother.

I told Katy to ask if there was anything else her mother wanted to share with her. Katy listened for a moment, and then a flood of tears flowed from her. Katy felt her mother close by, extending to her the love that Katy had felt she had been deprived of. Katy's guides knew that what would truly help her was to feel the love and support that she had never felt from her mother. It was not information that Katy needed. It was the emotional transformation that came with the connection with her mother's spirit.

The Mental Intuitives' Guides

A mental intuitive will want to ask questions. Mental intuitives want to know why, what, when, where, and how. They may want proof of the existence of a guide and may have trouble trusting that they are communicating with another life force. But our guides will not always respond to our need for proof and evidence. They seem to like to bring us into their reality, which we cannot easily measure by physical standards.

Mental intuitives will often dream of being in school or wake up tired, as if they have been learning all night. Mental intuitives are naturally telepathic and can attune themselves in meditation to their guide's vibration to receive guidance. Their guides tend to transfer information and knowledge to them at night or while they are daydreaming.

Mental intuitives will also be led to books, lectures, and other practical sources of information. Their guides will often sit beside them, encouraging them and guiding their soul evolution and education. Their guides may also set up experiences in their lives that we human beings cannot logically think our way through. On a path of understanding, mental intuitives are learning about the power of the mind, thought, and belief. Their guides who help them will not, however, answer all of their questions. They would rather set up experiences in which the answers that they seek will be revealed. Mental intuitives are on a quest for truth and discovery. Their guides might also have led physical lives driven by this desire.

Guides who work with mental intuitives often have distinct personalities and delight in being identified with a name. They can often be visualized by our inner sight, dressed in period clothing. They may have accomplished much on the physical plane, enjoy sharing and teaching what they have learned, and generally want to continue to be of assistance.

They can advance our knowledge on a larger scale than we can achieve by ourselves. Those working in the fields of medicine, technology, and science are being watched over by these devoted guides.

The guides of mental intuitives understand deeply those they help. They often work through humor and paradox, and create shifts in beliefs and patterns of thinking, to expand us beyond our limitations. They are able to conceive of a world in which science, technology, and medicine can solve the problems that have plagued us throughout time, and they wish to bring us into balance and wholeness. They work through the energy of the mind to create a life and world guided by wisdom and truth.

These guides dwell in the mental aura layer that is centered in our sixth chakra, also called the third eye. The third eye has the capability of transforming psychic energy into vision, an ability known as clairvoyance. Mental energy is constantly bombarding us. The reality that we experience in our day-to-day lives is usually driven by our mental beliefs and biases. As we transcend our normal self-centered view, the ability to see clairvoyantly also increases. Clairvoyance is the ability not just to see, but to see the truth.

As we evolve, our normal way of thinking is challenged. To enter into higher levels of consciousness, we must shed layers of ego and negativity. The reward of drawing from higher levels of consciousness is the ability to think beyond the confines of space and time. It is living, being, and thinking in the now. We are able to know beyond our ego.

Guides help us combine our mental and psychic energies, which creates a potent psychic strength that can transport us to the *Higher Mind*. This mind is what Deepak Chopra calls the realm of all possibilities within the unified field.[14] In this state of being, we connect with all of life and experience oneness. Gaining knowledge in the world is just the beginning of the journey. Our guides will lead us from simply knowing on a mental level into experiencing the results of cause and effect, and then guide us into transcendence. Our guides will lift us into the higher vibrations. In this higher state of being, we can become aware of an enlightened way of thinking. We can witness the creative force of our thoughts and be taught how to use our mental energy to create all that we desire.

Mental intuitives become empowered by grounding illuminated mental energy through the heart and then into physical manifestation. As our ability to transform mental energy increases, we begin to view life with wisdom and vision. We are called to lift our thoughts into the realm of all possibilities, the Divine Mind. When we do this, we are able to perceive that all of our life circumstances are opportunities for soul refinement and growth. We can learn the purpose and lesson that any situation has to teach us. Often when we accept the lessons we are to learn, our circumstances shift and our hardships pass.

Andy had always dreamed of owning his own business. After many years of working as a realtor for an established real estate business, he decided to venture out and start his own company. He was very ambitious. In addition to opening his own real estate business, he bought three apartment buildings with the thought of renovating and then reselling them. He invested all of his money and took out over a million dollars in loans.

Unfortunately, he encountered one obstacle after another. His properties were not selling, and he was not meeting his financial monthly demands. His accountant of many years was arrested for fraud. Consequently Andy was forced to go through lengthy, time-consuming audits with the IRS. Meanwhile, his identity was stolen, his credit was ruined, and if all this wasn't bad enough, he was being sued by one of his tenants. Andy was overwhelmed and devastated; he felt alone and unable to cope with the stress. Each day seemed worse than the one before. In his desperation Andy contemplated ending it all and committing suicide. He devised three ways to do so and began to plan out his demise. Andy's father had committed suicide when Andy was just three. Andy identified with his father as he felt he now understood him better. Andy planned to follow his father's example.

One evening, Andy sat with a gun in his hand. He felt ready to end it all, even resigned to his fate. Andy told me that it was at this moment that he heard a male voice shouting at him. He was alone, so he knew that the voice was not coming from a person—rather, it was a voice surrounding him, telling him to stop and to reconsider. Andy started a dialogue with this voice. The voice told him that he was Andy's guide and his name was Bernard. He told Andy in a calm English accent that there was no need to end his life, and he offered Andy his help.

Bernard explained to Andy that he would be able to help him get out of the financial mess he was in, but Andy would have to slow down, take one step at a time, and listen to his suggestions and open his mind to new ideas. Andy told Bernard that he was not inclined to trust a spirit named Bernard to help him out of such a huge financial mess. Bernard than told him that Andy would soon be meeting a man who would help him; he described what the man would look like in detail. Andy was intrigued by this prediction. He told Bernard that he reserved the right to end it all, but he was curious enough to wait a few days and see if Bernard was right.

A couple of weeks went by without the predicted meeting. Just as Andy was becoming disillusioned and more depressed, he decided to go to the bank and talk to his lender about his inability to make payments. While Andy waited for his lender, a man sitting in the waiting area with him struck up a conversation. The man talked about his desire to invest in real estate. He wanted to buy apartment buildings, to renovate and resell them. He even looked like the man Bernard had described. To say that Andy was surprised was an understatement. This man eventually bought one of Andy's properties and invested in Andy's business. Day by day things began to get better for Andy, and his relationship with Bernard became stronger. He took time and listened to him, following Bernard's guidance and suggestions.

Andy recently told me that he went to the home of a woman who was interested in listing her home with him. He told me that he talked at length with the woman, a half hour about real estate and two and a half hours about her spiritual life and her guides. Andy told me that with Bernard's help he showed her how to open herself to her guides' influence. Even though Andy and Bernard both have an interest in business, their connection far exceeds the mundane world. It is a relationship of trust, unconditional love, and wisdom.

The Spiritual Intuitive's Guides

Because spiritual intuitives can lift out of physical constraints with the greatest ease, they may enjoy connecting with their guides in the ethereal higher vibrations. Even while in the body, they sometimes consciously unite and merge with Spirit. They can do this so instinctively that they may not always be able to completely understand what is happening, but this will not detract from their experiencing a state of bliss.

The guides of a spiritual intuitive may belong to a soul group. A soul group is a congregation of individualized souls who join and vibrate together, communing with one another in a state of oneness. The energy of a soul group can be quite intense and stimulating; this energy can affect our healing and growth in a pronounced way. Spiritual guides tend to have less personality than guides in the mental and emotional realms and may lead a spiritual intuitive to poetry, prose, channeling, music, or chanting.

Because their influence will be felt as vibration, it takes some sensitivity to develop awareness of these guides. They enjoy working with people who also work in groups. We find spiritual intuitives in groups of people who meditate, chant, practice yoga, or worship together. They are community-minded and are teaching others to work together and create common goals. Spiritual intuitives are often perfecting the path of non-ego, and they attract guides who have transcended this limitation. It is difficult to know the names of these guides or visualize them in human form. They can be best connected to in ecstatic states and through the aura and energy field. Where the mental intuitive is working with the mind and the emotional intuitive with the heart, the spiritual intuitive is working with the energy field and aura. Spiritual intuitives are more sensitized to energy than the other types, and so their guides work with them through consciousness and sensation. Spiritual guides often will motivate their Earth friends through inspirational shifts of awareness and feelings of upliftment.

One of the gifts that the spiritual intuitive brings to Earth is the ability to energize the planet with spiritual energy. They are transformers and mystical alchemists with the ability to infuse the physical with vital life, giving waves from pure source. Many of the guides and teachers that work with them have not had Earth lives. They may be souls who have inhabited other planets and celestial systems. It is also likely that spiritual intuitives have not had many Earth lives themselves, and their guides are often companions from other worlds. The common link between a spiritual intuitive and their guides is the experience of nonphysical reality.

Spiritual guides work through our higher chakras—the seventh, eighth, and beyond, where the spiritual intuitive is centered. Spiritual intuitives tend not to like boundaries and the feeling of confinement, and they often feel their consciousness expanding beyond the physical. They live more in their energy field and less in their physical bodies, and so their guides communicate with them primarily through essence. Spiritual intuitives absorb information through the aura, which is one reason why they can have trouble putting into words what their experience may be. When we receive psychic information through the energy field, we feel it as sensation, an inner vibration that can be stimulating and inspiring. Translating psychic energy into the physical takes skill. It can also be tiring on the physical body.

Spiritual intuitives do not always feel as if they have a strong connection to the physical world. Many regard being here as necessary for their karma—a steppingstone before the ultimate transcendence into spirit—and they are likely to escape into the higher realms whenever possible. Spiritual intuitives have the ability to help others shift into higher spiritual states. They are capable of channeling miraculous healings and genius works of art and music. To do all this, they need to commit to being here in the physical, not just hanging out in spirit. Their work is to transform higher spiritual energy into the heavier physical vibration. Their guides can lower the intensity of the spiritual vibration to combine with the physical. Guides do this in order to make contact with their physical companions and to assist them in their more material concerns. Just because they are more closely aligned with essence and the nonphysical realities does not mean that these guides are not able to work within the framework of the physical. They can help their earthbound friends to create abundance and to manifest the lives that they desire.

Spiritual intuitives often get an overwhelming sense of knowing. They will not know how or why they know, but they know. Along with these deep feelings of knowing often come profound spiritual understanding and insight. Spiritual intuitives are likely to receive energy from higher levels of perception. They seem to have an easier time connecting with people who have passed into spirit. More than the other types they will dream of those who have departed the physical and be able to communicate with them in both the dream state and while awake. They can elevate their consciousness to make contact with nonphysical energy with ease, often without full awareness of what they are doing.

Beth has many guides. They enjoy her very much. Beth feels her guides as waves of warmth and soothing streams of colors. She goes on wonderful spiritual adventures with her spiritual companions while in deep meditation. Beth and her spirit friends soul travel to various multidimensional planes, gliding in rich warm waves of ecstatic vibrations.

When Beth came in for a reading, she was concerned about her finances and her health. Although Beth seemed naturally attuned to her abundant spiritual energy, she was having challenges with the more down-to-earth aspects of life. Similar to many spiritual intuitives, she assumed that her guides were like her. She thought they were wonderful as mystical companions but would be of little help when it came to the practical aspects of her life.

But her guides, like most guides, do not regard our physical lives as unspiritual or out of the realm of their influence. Not living in duality, they actually can affect our mundane lives in surprising ways. They work to help us to live without the limitations and restrictions to which we bind ourselves. Beth's guides wanted her to ask for their help and guidance in the more ordinary parts of her life. When I communicated this to her, she seemed taken aback. She had a hard time feeling that the spiritual and the physical could be aligned in her life. Beth felt that her guides could not help her and were not interested in the material part of her life. There was for her a clear division between the spiritual and the material realms.

Beth has a purpose in this life. She is working toward experiencing her heaven on Earth. To do this, she needs to suspend her judgments. She cannot specify some things in her life as spiritual and some things as not spiritual. It is all spirit manifesting through the physical. She has to allow the grace of her Higher Self to be expressed. She can flourish as a spiritual being in the physical world. Her guides know this. They are with her to help her.

The Physical Intuitive's Guides

Physical intuitives connect best with more earth-based guides such as animal, plant, mineral, and water spirits, and spirits who work in the shamanic and Devic worlds. They may also enjoy the company of supernatural beings like elementals, fairies, elves, and gods and goddesses such as Pan and Isis. Their guides can be magicians and expert alchemists who seek to share their abilities with their well-loved human apprentices.

Many earth-based guides tend to show up in the physical world and are likely to appear to us in familiar forms. They are at home in and on the earth and are likely to have had highly evolved lives on the earth. They may have been leaders within Native American, Mayan, Aztec, Atlantean, Celtic, Egyptian, and Peruvian cultures, to name a few. They have a great love for the earth and inspire the physical intuitive to listen to and speak with the wisdom of the earth. These guides are usually adept at working within the confines of material matter. They have the ability to take on form at will and they can alter and shape physical phenomena. They may be the butterfly on our windowsill, the cloud shaping itself into the shape of a cherub, a crystal that intensifies our psychic ability, or a stranger on the road whose smile transforms our day.

Steven has many animal guides. He also has many pets. He has dogs, cats, birds, even a donkey. Since childhood, he has had a special affinity for blue jays, which were the first animals he felt he could communicate with. Blue jays often show up in his life at times of change or transition. One summer he found three dead blue jays at different times close to his home. That same summer his mother passed into spirit and his wife had a miscarriage. Later that fall he left a job that he had had for a number of years.

Steven told me that as he found the blue jays, one by one, he knew that they were bringing him a message, foretelling losses. When these losses occurred, he had a sense of spiritual presence. The lifeless bodies of the blue jays had helped him to accept the transitions that were to come. He felt that they had cared for him enough to pass into spirit so they could prepare and forewarn him of changes to come.

Residing close to nature and the earth and considering the natural world their heaven and their home, the guides of a physical intuitive often take pleasure in ceremony and ritual. They enjoy and honor new moon ceremonies, Wiccan spells, solstice celebrations, and medicine wheel observances. These guides inhabit the seas, the stones, and the grasses that surround us. They work on the earth plane through energetic vortexes like those found in Sedona, Arizona and in other locations in the Americas, Europe, and all over the world. Part of their mission is to purify the earth. They do this by helping to release negative and stuck energy patterns. Like their guides, physical intuitives have the innate desire to transform the harmful and toxic aspects of our environment into a pristine and divine haven. The guides of physical intuitives sometimes inhabit plants and flowers with the intent of offering healing to the human and animal world.

∼∼∼∼∼

Better than the other types, physical intuitives can become aware of the inner spirit that resides within the physical. They are more able to perceive nature spirits, communicate with animals, and perceive God in nature. Rarely does the modern world honor and pay tribute to the innate wisdom of the earth, but the physical intuitive easily communes with the spirit made physical.

Earth-based spiritual traditions such as Wicca and those practiced by Native Americans seek insight into the mystery of life and death through the cycles of nature. The earth is the schoolhouse for physical intuitives, as they interact instinctually and naturally with the simplicity of the natural world. They gain insight into the meaning of life through the beauty of the stars and skies. They often seek to manifest their desires by working in unison with the spirits in nature. The physical intuitives' guides are teaching them to harmonize their physical energy with the supernatural, which will enable them to influence the creation of their ideal outcomes.

We tend to think of guides as ethereal and unearthly. The guides of physical intuitives can appear to be tangible and solid, but this is only temporary. They will reside no more than momentarily in the entity, creature, or natural object that appeals to them. They delight in play and like to trick us and have fun with us. They can unsettle us. We will begin to question what we view as "real" and "solid."

The guides of a physical intuitive often work in a different manner than other guides do. Instead of going within ourselves to communicate with these guides, we will often find them in the external world. Sometimes they show up in the body of a cat or a dog that suddenly appears on our doorstep. They may stay a day or a few years; they will be with you as long as they need to be in order to fulfill whatever it is that they have come to teach. These guides can teach us to shapeshift, to alter and transform the physical body. They call us to view ourselves beyond the physical limitations that we perceive as reality. They vibrate to and love the physical, but they are not bound to it. They wish to teach us to weave our consciousness in and out of the physical.

A physical intuitive may be slower than others to explore new technologies, spiritual schools, or abstract ideas. Their guides often motivate them through an interest in Earth phenomena. Extraordinary phenomena—including extraterrestrials, the mysterious Bermuda Triangle, the ancient Atlantis civilization, and ghosts—attract the curiosity of many physical intuitives. These interests can become a doorway for their guides to further influence the physical intuitive's growth and awareness by drawing them deeper into the wonder of life.

Physical intuitives have a tendency to absorb energy from the environment in their physical bodies, which can cause them added stress. The guides of physical intuitives will help bring conscious awareness to the vibrations of energy that they might be holding in their bodies. They do this by setting up situations in which the physical intuitive will feel, experience, and respond. Their guides will work to get them talking, singing, chanting, and feeling.

Angela has been a social worker for over twenty years in the rural county where she grew up. Over the course of her career, Angela has worked with infants, children, adults, and seniors. She has always played an important role in her family of origin. Her father has a debilitating mental illness, and her mother has for years battled an addiction to alcohol and prescription drugs. Angela has a brother a few years younger than herself.

Angela grew up taking care of her brother and the rest of the family. Given the caretaking role that she grew up with, her expertise and proficiency as a social worker is no surprise. Angela has been in chronic pain for many years; her joints ache and she suffers from fibromyalgia. She has tried various medical and holistic treatments, searching for something that will release her from chronic pain. She has experienced different levels of relief from time to time, but the pain persists in varying degrees. There are days when Angela feels so rundown and tired that all she can manage is to sit quietly in her garden, absorbing the sun's rays and enjoying the flowers and plants. She looks forward to these times; she feels soothed and comforted while in the presence of the natural world.

Angela remembers the small yard of her childhood home, where she often went to get away from the yelling and tension inside her home. While outside, Angela would play make-believe with the fairies and magical beings that she imagined lived in the nooks and crannies of the plants and trees. Some of them were fun and made her laugh; others liked to play tricks and hide the little knick-knacks that she played with. She knew that she couldn't talk to her parents or other grownups about them, as the fairies scolded her one day after she dragged her mother off the couch to join her in playing with them. They would only play with *her*, they told Angela. The others were too loud and annoying. Angela played with her garden friends during the challenging first seven years of her life, eventually moving from this home into an apartment.

During a recent visit to her garden, Angela dozed off in her lounge chair, and a few minutes later awoke to a peculiar melodic song she remembered from her childhood playing in her ear. She instinctively hummed along with it. To her amazement she remembered the different verses and most of the words. As she hummed along, flashes of color coming from behind some bushes quickly raced in front of her half-open eyes. Maybe they have returned, she thought, those nature spirits and fairies who used to dance and sing along with her as a child. She was skeptical that they were even "real," though. They were just imaginary playmates invented from her loneliness, she told herself. Still, she smiled and felt warmly comforted by the thought that they had found her.

Angela came out to the garden more often after this, watching, waiting for more signs that she was not alone. Angela began to leave small colorful stones and ribbons, remembering their fondness for trinkets. She hoped to entice them to visit her, make themselves visible. Angela continued to do this for many months. She began to read more about these earth spirits, being drawn in by the possibility of their existence. This brought her a sense of serenity and peace; she felt less alone than she had in long time.

Over time Angela has continued her garden fairy watch. They have again become her companions, drawing her into their world of color, fun, pleasure, and simple amusement. It doesn't matter so much to Angela if there is ever solid proof of their existence. She knows, by the missing colored stones or the neatly laid ribbon that greets her in the morning, that her friends are close.

Our guides and angels can significantly affect our lives. We are rarely aware of the surprising ways in which they lead us to grow and evolve. Physical intuitives live with the memory of a pure Earth buried deep within them; their friends in spirit work to awaken them to this rich inner knowing.

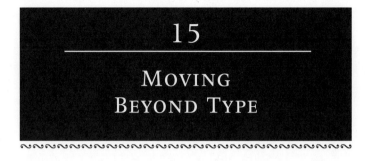

15

MOVING
BEYOND TYPE

Once we become aware which of the four intuitive types we are, and give attention and energy to this part of ourselves, our intuitive preferences will begin to evolve. If we become too rigid and focused in one modality, our growth can become stifled and stunted. It is thus important to honor and see the value in paths other than our own, instead of getting locked into the perception that Spirit is a certain way.

Emotional intuitives can believe that finding the perfect soul mate or love is the path to perfection. They can spend their lives in search of their soul mate and the ideal love relationship. Mental intuitives can believe that understanding the *what* and *who* of God is the only way. They may require scientific proof to believe in spiritual realities. Spiritual intuitives may not be able to connect with their purpose on Earth and live out their spiritual ideals. They may wander aimlessly in and out of various spiritual practices, never integrating their heightened spiritual awareness into their daily lives. They may reject the material world as shallow and meaningless. Physical intuitives may lack motivation to grow and understand their own multidimensional potential. They might not see the value of spiritual realities, or discount them altogether and live a purely material-centered life.

Our guides can help us to evolve beyond our biases. I first became aware of divination through an old I Ching book that I came across in high school. I was fascinated by this book of ancient Chinese wisdom. The I Ching teaches the path to spiritual attainment and good fortune using metaphors of nature to illustrate the laws of the universe. We learn its lessons by throwing three coins six times to form a hexagram, which, when interpreted, illustrates the present situation that we may find ourselves in and gives advice on the best way to proceed.

I loved to throw the coins and see what the I Ching had to say to me. I would read and reread the advice the hexagram offered. This started me on a path that led me to consulting with various metaphysical practitioners and astrologers, and an interest in all kinds of paranormal phenomena. During this time, many of the psychics I saw told me that I had a particular Catholic saint as a guide. This was interesting to me, but it didn't make much sense. I was brought up as a Protestant. My mother was a Methodist minister, and I had no idea why a Catholic saint would be hanging out with me.

Saints were foreign to my past and far from my current interests. After having been told this a few times, however, I decided to find out more about this saint. When I discovered that she was known for her loving, simple nature and her devotion to Jesus, I was even more perplexed. Why would she be guiding me? What did she want to teach me? I would try to send her the message that I appreciated her attention, but I thought she had the wrong person.

It took many years and a lot of influence from this loving guide for me to realize my own deep emotional nature. I was more comfortable in the spiritual realms, and it was easier for me to understand an abstract spiritual book like the I Ching than it was to imagine a loving saint close by. I had no true emotional understanding of myself at that time. I was making errors in life that were causing me emotional distress and pain. While I also felt deeply for others, I did not have the emotional maturity to know how to express my deep emotional and spiritual ideals. I have learned the most about Spirit through a heartfelt path, yet at that time I was most attracted to more esoteric expressions of spirituality. Had I not been led into the energy of the heart, I would have not integrated my unknown potential.

Many people who actively desire spiritual growth and ask for guidance from Spirit find that at a certain point they begin to have experiences that make them feel uncomfortable. Spirit's plan is not always the same as our plan. Part of our growth will be to expand our understanding beyond our initial perception. The shift from our natural intuitive strength to the development of other intuitive perspectives is not always easy or comfortable.

Often we are only willing to go beyond our limitations when we are unsatisfied with the present state of things. It may be that we are driven by a desire for a different job, better health, more money, or a love relationship. Some people are also interested in learning their purpose or mission in life, and others have a greater sense of their spiritual identity and would like to connect with loved ones in spirit or enhance their psychic ability. Our desires thus motivate the choices we make.

On the spiritual level, our Higher Self and our guides use desire to move us out of resistance. Our ego normally fears change and attempts to control our life, those around us, and our environment. Trying to avoid change, we allow inertia to set in, and with inertia come boredom and (possibly) depression. But when we long for something that we feel we are lacking, then we are more willing to allow change into our lives. Desire can be a path that leads us to seek the truth. Of course, desire fueled by a lack of understanding can also lead us into striving to find happiness outside of ourselves. We have to evolve in order to manifest what we desire. We become or grow into what we are seeking.

Laura

During the past several years, Laura has taken many intuition development classes. She wants to help people. She would like to develop her intuitive abilities to such a degree that she will be able to give psychic messages and guidance to others, but right now she is very frustrated by what she feels is her lack of progress. Laura has read, studied, practiced, and meditated, and still she feels no more psychic or intuitive than she did before she began this journey.

Laura has her own marketing company. She is financially successful and admired by many in her field for her many business accomplishments, but still she strives to become psychic. She would like to walk away from her business and began anew as a spiritual counselor. Laura is also very frustrated with me. She asks me questions such as *Why does God give others this gift and not me? What do I have to do to become more psychic? Why is this not working?*

Laura has approached intuitive development the same way that she approaches projects in the business world. She takes classes and does the work, the reading, and the studying. She struggles to fit the spiritual world into the realm where she is most comfortable. Unlike most of our worldly pursuits and occupations, however, psychic development requires that we evolve on many levels. Intuition calls us into parts of ourselves that may be dormant and unused. Intuitive growth is about listening within. We have to be able to hear what our soul is asking of us. And it is important to remember that our soul is not a thing. It is not an academic subject that we can master and control. No, it is just the opposite. Our soul is alive and has intelligence, power, wisdom, and beauty. It lives within us, connecting us to God, the divine source. When we listen to its voice, we will be led to our bliss. But to hear its small quiet voice, we need to open ourselves and expand beyond what we know or think we know.

Laura's intuitive style is obviously centered in her mental energy. Although she has learned many things and developed herself in mental intuition, she needs to go beyond this modality. She is now learning to access her intuition in a more spiritual way. She is meditating, listening, and immersing herself in divine energy as a spiritual intuitive does. She is disciplining herself to give up the goal and live in the moment. This is not easy for her. She wants to see results. She wants to be an accurate psychic who can give specific information to others. The thought of hanging out with Spirit and merely experiencing energy does not appeal to her. In order to receive the psychic information that she desires, however, she needs to learn to be an open channel. Focusing on the ethereal, the unknown, and the intangible will heighten her intuitive sensors.

While our guides may be loving and compassionate, they will not be able to keep us from the effects of our beliefs and judgments. Intuitive energy is balanced and unbiased. Our intuition may be more accurate when it comes in along avenues where we are clearest and most impartial. For many people, these avenues are in their nondominant modalities. Our material-focused ego also tends to be more involved when we work through our strengths. Intuition is the connection with the soul, the inner voice. The ego is not objective. It rarely sees things clearly. It usually works to strengthen itself; it is fear-based and seeks to have power over and dominate our more soulful aspirations.

Intuition is the merging of our consciousness with the greater whole. The ego cannot accomplish this merging. It is for this reason that we will tend to make more spiritual progress in those parts of ourselves where our ego feels less competent. To more fully reach our potential, we have to learn to inhabit terrain that may be unfamiliar to us. If we react with fear or aversion to different ways of relating to ourselves and the world, we can create inner disharmony. We will manifest these imbalances in some way. The law of attraction states that what we experience in life is a direct manifestation of our beliefs and thoughts. If we make judgments about others, we may find ourselves being judged and criticized by others. Our greatest psychic growth will occur when we open ourselves and go beyond the limitations of our self-centered viewpoints and perceptions.

Eric

Since childhood, Eric has been interested in learning all he can about extraterrestrials and life forms on other planets. He has read and studied books, and attended workshops and conferences, to learn all he can about the subject. He feels that his mind has been opened to a vast world of knowledge that he readily enjoys. When Eric was recently diagnosed with cancer, he followed his customary path and began researching various forms of healing. He sought out traditional and alternative health methods, read the research, and talked to many people. He became a knowledge base for others interested in alternatives and options for healing.

Eric regularly saw both an oncologist and a variety of alternative practitioners, one of whom suggested that he attend a meditation workshop. Eric went, hopeful that the workshop would help reduce his stress level. He knew through his reading that meditation has beneficial results for stress reduction. He was given time during the workshop to be quiet, to meditate, to listen within. During his meditation, feelings and emotions welled up and he became aware of intense feelings buried deep within him. It felt to him as if a faucet had been opened inside, and grief, sadness, and fear were pouring out.

As these deep emotions surfaced, Eric began to weep. For what felt to him like hours, he felt the intensity of his feelings and allowed them to be expressed. Others in the workshop comforted him and allowed him his space. They expressed compassion and understanding. Eric emerged from the workshop feeling cleansed, clear, and loved. He had not known that he needed this emotional type of healing and felt that he had received a great gift. It was a healing as important as the physical healing he was seeking.

Eric is a mental intuitive. He pursued the path of healing through learning, study, and application, but it was in his emotional energy that he was blocked. When he allowed himself to enter into this part of himself, he felt immediately relieved.

This is true for most of us. While we would rather stay where we feel competent and safe, a great deal of the healing and growth that we desire occurs in the areas where we are least comfortable. It is often in the parts of ourselves that we consider least important or useful that our potency for change and growth lies.

Growing with Our Guides

Although we tend to come into intuitive work in our comfort zone, we are assisted and helped by guides and higher divine energies whose vision far exceeds our limitations. Their purpose is far greater than we might think. While we usually are centered in our needs and desires, our spiritual helpers see the big picture. They know the power that lies within us. They see us not just from the human perspective but also from the divine, and they invest in us not only to increase our joy and understanding but also for the betterment of the world.

When we are ready, we attract guides who teach us to go beyond our limitations. They often have more confidence in us than we have in ourselves and in our ability to learn in new ways. They teach us by setting up situations where we are forced to shift our view. This can happen in a variety of ways. We may find ourselves romantically attracted to someone very different from us. We might have been born into a family whose views and beliefs about life differ from ours. We might find ourselves in a work environment where we feel odd and misunderstood.

These situations can be uncomfortable and even painful, but they force us to feel and know how others feel and know. The less judgmental we are of others, the easier it is to change ourselves and grow. It can be difficult to embrace a perspective that seems strange or foreign. The intuitive life can lead us into experiences and situations that motivate and stimulate these changes.

16

CLEARING THE
PSYCHIC CHANNELS

~~~~~~

The unbalanced spiritual ego is that part of our consciousness that seeks to separate from the whole, from the "all that is," and from our complete union with oneness. It is a willful aspect of our nature that feels that our spiritual beliefs are more valid or real than what others believe or practice. Sometimes people are drawn to psychic and intuitive work as a way to access information and knowledge in order to feel superior to others. It can be tempting to believe that having intuitive insight makes one special and closer to the truth. Spiritual egotism is a danger that our guides and angels work to help us to avoid.

It is not uncommon for us to become overly focused on our personal wants and desires because the world we live in tends to create a self-centered attitude. We are taught to work hard to control ourselves and others. Each day, we add more stress and worry to our already overburdened lives. Not believing that we exist within a consistent flow of love and abundance, we compete with one another in what appears to be a zero-sum environment. Our guides and other helpers attempt to create experiences for us that will lift us into higher levels of consciousness. They work to enable us to experience our power to co-create and draw to us our good. When we come to the realization that our ego actually gets in the way of our joy and prosperity, we will be more willing to ignore its chattering voice. To enter into a life of grace, we must believe that grace exists—that grace is as authentic and powerful as the tangible, concrete world that we define as real.

Intuitive development will, at some point, take us out of ourselves and expand our understanding of others' perspectives and realities. It ought to be a path out of narcissism and into oneness.

Each intuitive type might experience this process somewhat differently. Emotional intuitives will be led by love and service to others. Their spiritual path takes them from the self-absorption of co-dependent love to the experience of unconditional love. Emotional intuitives are on a journey into the heart of wisdom and compassion, transforming painful emotions into clear insight.

Mental intuitives are centered in the mind. They are being led to the experience of Divine Mind and sharing the thoughts of God. They may have to discipline their mind to accept ideas and thoughts from the vibrations of wisdom, always willing to be nonjudgmental and open to new possibilities. They will have to question the accepted thought patterns that may keep them bound to negativity and narrow-mindedness.

Physical intuitives live the path of the divine manifesting in and through the physical. They are very much in the body and on the earth, and their journey is from duality to oneness. The experience of no division between what is of body and what is of spirit is their deepest lesson. Physical intuitives will move from duality to oneness by becoming more aware of subtle energies and not discounting realities that are not in physical form. They will evolve in their journey as they accept the intangible and become better able to perceive the ethereal within themselves and the world around them.

Spiritual intuitives are somewhat similar, but they work from the opposite direction, as they live in spirit yet are bound to the physical. Their path is the experience of freedom. For spiritual intuitives, embodying oneness is the ability to fully live their spiritual purpose here on Earth. It is to bring the magic and inspiration of their spirit fully into the physical. They are here to learn to share their truth fully in the physical without judgment and restriction. When they commit to a plan of action and see their purpose manifest in the world, they will be able to fully integrate their spirit with the physical.

Our guides and angels will usually initiate our learning process. As our trust in the connection that we have with our guides, angels, and other teachers becomes stronger and more tangible, we will be led into deeper psychic waters. We will question less our nonphysical connections and begin to rely and depend more on the guidance we are receiving. As our connection with Spirit deepens, our intuition will become not only a tool to understand the events of our daily lives, but it will also shift our understanding of reality. We will begin to see beyond our self-centered material concerns. We will begin to find our security within. We will begin to rely more on the unseen.

Each intuitive type will be challenged by its innate strengths. This is because the ego is full of pride in its achievements. But the psychic journey to wholeness is about *inner healing*. We cannot clearly read or intuit energies outside of ourselves until we attain inner clarity.

Cassie

For years, Cassie has taken classes to develop the ability to be a medium. She has always been attracted to spiritual pursuits and helping others. She is an ordained Methodist minister, but she worked in the church for only a few years; she presently works as the director of a hospice where people rely on her empathy and skill at helping others to cope in times of crisis.

Cassie recently took a psychic development class of mine. During the class exercises, she was surprised by the emergence of some old, deep-rooted childhood pain that surfaced during a meditation. She felt overwhelmed by the intensity and the depth of the sadness that seemed to explode within her. After class, she asked me why this had happened. She told me that her intent was to develop as a medium and said she felt disappointed that instead of connecting with people who had passed over, she instead felt her own inner pain. Her emotional energy was blocked.

Cassie is an emotional intuitive, and in order for her to be able to open to the voice of spirit and intuit the energy of others, it is necessary for her to become a clear channel. We cannot bypass our own growth. Cassie did not like feeling her own deep emotions when her guides had led her not to intuiting the energy of others but to her own place of need. In a way, she felt betrayed. Cassie came into class with a high degree of empathy. For a long time she has worked assisting other people in painful situations, and in the process she has become adept at handling emotional intensity. Even though Cassie is very competent in dealing with the emotions of others, in the intuition development class she found herself confronting her own buried pain.

In order for Cassie to move deeper into her psychic potential, she needs to learn to transform painful emotions and release herself from any inner emotional toxicity. This can be difficult work, but when we undertake this deep and inner transformative activity, powerful spiritual inner gateways open. We become free to love from the deep source of unconditional love within us, to embrace the heart of wisdom unencumbered by the static and self-centeredness of our wounds, and to open a clear path for psychic energy to flow. Our pain cries out for attention and drives our consciousness into behaviors that it believes will bring healing and wholeness. Yet when we deny our wounds, we often act out our unconscious pain in confusing and self-defeating ways. We only attract those experiences that reinforce our suffering. Eventually our pain must be released and transformed.

Tammy

I had a client, Tammy, who had not dated for many years, but she had recently posted a singles ad on an Internet dating site. Tammy was a wonderful writer and a very attractive woman. Her entertaining ad received over thirty responses from men from all walks of life—among them were engineers, scientists, construction workers, software developers, attorneys, and a chef. She met most of the men and slowly narrowed the dating prospects to three or four. From these men she eventually decided to exclusively date one man, Henry. Tammy felt strongly that he was "the one."

After a few months of dating Henry, Tammy called me, very upset. She told me that she had not heard from Henry in over a week; he had not answered her phone calls and he had not been to work. She was convinced that something had happened to him. She was seeking out his friends and co-workers, trying to find out anything she could. In the process she discovered that Henry had gone on a drinking binge; he was at home in his bed, drunk and despondent. Tammy was devastated. She did not even know that he drank. What surprised her in a way even more was that this was the same pattern that her father would fall into when she was young. He would work hard, be attentive, and then periodically he would go on a drinking binge that would sometimes last for weeks. She remembered times when no one would know where he was for days.

We re-create our wounds in order to heal them. Our conscious mind is usually unaware that we are doing so, yet what drives our behavior is what lurks within us that is in need of healing. Our spiritual ego is often tied up in our pain. It is our ego that has been wounded. When we heal the pain, the spiritual ego begins to dissolve. When our ego is in charge of our intuitive and psychic development, we will be plagued by over-striving and worry. We will never do enough, never be enough. We will encounter frustration and self-judgment. We may believe that we are more special, more powerful than others, but this path leads nowhere. Our karma will suffer and our ability to connect with the higher healing energies will be diminished. No angels and divine guides will come to our assistance.

Whatever intuitive type we may be, eventually we will find that our past wounds, pains, blocks, and unevolved human parts will surface. This is good, as it gives us the opportunity to become free and to live in the present. We can ask our angels, guides, and teachers to help us to unblock our painful, wounded parts. Powerful, loving angels are ready to carry our hurt and wounds into the Light, where these heavy energies can be transformed. When we ask, we can be showered within with healing white light. Wherever we have held pain and negativity can become a vessel of love and forgiveness. This kind of healing infuses our spiritual psychic growth with fresh, clear, vibrant energy. As we receive lush, warm waves of wisdom, guidance and love will be able to be a beckon of love and wisdom for others.

Our soul is untarnished, untouched, and unaffected by all that comes our way. When we gain knowledge of the power of our soul to assist our healing and to attract higher energies that fill us with radiance, we come closer to acknowledging our true identity. We will then live our lives less fearful of outcomes and our need to control every aspect of our lives will diminish. We can rest. We can listen. It is our soul that is connected to the Divine Mind and the wise and compassionate heart. It is our soul that is psychic. It is to our soul that our guides and higher energies speak.

17

SHIFTING INTO HIGHER AWARENESS

~~~~~~

Our spirit longs to wake us up to see the psychic sea of all that is. We may begin this passage with an increase in dreams or premonitions that involve others, often our family or friends. We may get immediate impressions upon meeting new people or going to new places. We may feel as if we might have been given a message or important information to give to someone. Often when we begin to have these experiences, our initial response is to wonder why we have been given access to knowing particular extrasensory information. For some people, a psychic opening-up can be upsetting. They feel silly or awkward letting others know that they have had a dream or intuitive impression that might relate to them.

Getting intuitive impressions can be like soaking up the rays of the sun. Energy is always circulating and as we begin to open, it is normal for us to pick up anything that is being energetically broadcast. We may not always understand why and how we have received certain psychic information. It is not uncommon to have a psychic breakthrough that involves an unfortunate or traumatic event. These are deviations from the natural flow of energy. Even though we usually do not feel as if we are psychically attuned to our environment, when there is an energetic disorder we are likely to pick up on it.

Some people may "know," "see," or "feel" premonitions of plane crashes, earth changes, or other disturbing future events. They may try in vain to alert others, even calling airports or disaster-preparedness organizations and voicing their concerns and impressions. These are usually discounted, even laughed at, causing the intuitive receiver even more distress. Many people will attempt to shut down their psychic abilities for this reason.

Unexpected Intuitive Benefits

Most people begin to understand that as their intuition deepens, they have the ability to help not only themselves but to help others as well. We do not always know how to do this, though; it can take time to find the best outlet for our psychic energy. There is a sense of peace and connection that comes when we find a path for our emerging psychic personality. When we can give without a selfish aim, we begin to flourish and feel an inner sense of joy. As their spiritual and intuitive path expands, most people become less self-centered and more concerned with being of service to others. This may be because our intuition becomes stronger and clearer when our focus is to be of assistance to others. Often, once we have a sense of how we can connect with others and the world in a beneficial way, our intuitive ability begins to flourish. Our intuitive and psychic growth can then deepen, taking us into even more profound inner transformations. As these inner changes progress, our ability to be an accurate psychic will also evolve.

Often we are not even aware of how we may be being used by Spirit to help others. Our friends, family, and even strangers might be led to seek out our advice or opinion during difficult times. When we remain open and connected to our spiritual inner voice, we often have the power to positively affect others without even knowing it. The paradox is that as we allow ourselves to be of benefit to others, our own lives improve. More goodness comes our way. When we know that we are connected to the universal All That Is, and that there is a beautiful design of love and wisdom guiding our lives, our stresses and anxieties lessen. We can then operate more clearly and be guided to make better choices.

A few years ago I led a ten-month psychic/spiritual development class. We met once a month for four hours on Sunday afternoons. During the first class I asked the thirty-two participants to write down what they would like to have manifest in their lives by the end of the ten months. Anything was possible. Some people wanted to lose weight or improve their health. A few wanted a better job or to change their career to an occupation that was more satisfying. Others desired to be involved in a loving relationship, and some people wanted to improve the relationship that they were in. Only two people wanted to become a proficient psychic or medium.

I collected the papers and held on to them for the ten months. We did not directly work on any of the desires. My focus in the class was instead to help individuals to better understand their intuitive abilities, to increase their confidence, and to give them an opportunity to intuitively help one another. At the last class I handed out the papers and one by one we read them. Most people had forgotten what they wrote, yet all but a few people had achieved their intended desire.

The most surprising change might have been from Beth, a woman in her fifties who had never been married and had not dated for over a decade. She wrote during the first class that she wanted to be married or to be in a committed relationship. She called me a few months after the class ended and told me that during the time of the class she had met a man at a dinner party thrown by some co-workers. This man was a widower, who had a few years before lost his wife after a long illness. They struck up a conversation about psychic things, in which they both had an interest, and they talked with ease well into the night. Beth told me that she felt she was falling in love with him, and she wanted me to give her a reading to tell her if he was the one. She questioned her own inner knowing that this was the real thing, she told me, because she never thought that this could happen for her. To say that she was surprised would be an understatement.

The Deepening Path

What unfolds in life can sometimes be a gentle process, but often it is not. We can sometimes feel like the victim of life's ups and downs, or blessed by a variety of loving, helpful influences. We might at times feel as if the hand that we have been dealt is unfair and cruel. Sometimes it can be easy to distrust the spiritual, and to see it as mystifying and without reason. We judge ourselves by what occurs in life because we are not always able to understand the deeper lessons that we draw to ourselves. We do this from a soul level, and our conscious self may be bewildered by what is happening. Some people find themselves thrust into a life that seems beyond their ability to cope.

Yet the true joy of Spirit often springs from that which seems the most difficult. As the Persian spiritual poet and theologian Rumi once wrote:

> *The way of love is not*
> *a subtle argument.*
> *The door there*
> *is devastation.*
> *Birds make great sky-circles*
> *of their freedom.*
> *How do they learn it?*
> *They fall, and falling,*
> *they're given wings.* [15]

We have a choice to view the events in our life as random and circumstantial, or as part of a plan for our highest good. Our intuitive development can help us to stay connected to the deeper meaning of what occurs in our lives. We can never truly judge the circumstances that we and others go through. We are not flawed—nor are we less loved or less worthy—if our circumstances in life have been challenging. Our soul may have orchestrated a life abundant with difficulties so that we might quickly be drawn to seek solace in the spiritual. We are brought to the doorway of the divine by many different paths.

Donna

For many people, the unexpected death of a loved one catapults them into an awareness of life that they never knew existed. Donna's husband Mark was a skilled thoracic surgeon who worked long hours at the local hospital. One Saturday morning after a grueling week of long days and nights, he woke early and headed to the golf course for a day of golf with friends. He was found a few hours later, sitting in his parked car, dead of a massive heart attack. He was a man who had helped and healed so many, yet at the age of just forty-nine his life was over.

Donna felt that Mark was her soul mate, that they could share a deep, divine love. But their marriage was a difficult one. Mark worked long hours, and so Donna never felt that she was enjoying the kind of love with Mark that she had always longed for. Her suffering after his death was not only for the loss of him, but also for the loss of what she felt she was never fully able to experience with him. Donna had always believed that one day they would share the kind of love that she dreamed of. For her, the desire for partnership and deep sharing with her soul mate was the ultimate testimony of life. When Mark died, her dreams seemed to be shattered.

Donna and Mark had two children, a son and a daughter, and Donna now became both mother and father to them. She worked in the home and outside of it. Their son, Sam, had been born with digestive and intestinal-tract problems and had numerous surgeries when very young. The surgeries had been successful, and Donna worked tirelessly to help her son during his healing. She poured her heart and soul into caring for him. After his father's death, Sam, then seventeen, became addicted to drugs. Donna found a residential treatment program for him. Again she focused on his care with total dedication and devotion. After a long, tough stay in treatment, Sam learned to deal with his addiction. He stopped using and began to have hope for the future. He healed and became strong. On his twenty-second birthday, on his way to the beach to celebrate with friends, Sam died in a motorcycle accident.

It had been barely a year since her son's death when Donna came into our session quiet and withdrawn. She wanted to communicate with Sam, so we began the session by connecting with him in spirit. He was very close, very emotional. He loved his mother very much. During the hour we talked, her mother, father, husband, and son, all in spirit, drew close and sought to ease Donna's pain.

At the end of the session, Donna asked me for help in getting through this difficult time. She wondered how she could ever go on in life. She had loved her husband and her son. They were gone. She felt as if her life had ended. I told Donna that I knew there was no getting through this kind of loss. A part of her was now in spirit. Her life was forever altered.

Donna now lives in two worlds. Her joy, peace, and serenity depend on her acceptance of the unseen in her life. Her relations and her heart in part now exist in essence, not in the physical, tangible world. The more she develops her spiritual awareness, the stronger and more comfortable she will feel. It had always been her desire to experience the ultimate union of her soul in deep love with another. It may now be that this wish will be fulfilled in spirit. It is through the awareness of the spiritual intuitive's orientation that she will be able to actualize her heart's desire. I asked her to try not to think of her son and husband as dead. They have been resurrected, reborn in spirit. A part of Donna died when they died. That part of her has also been resurrected and has been reborn. She has an open door to the other side. Her path has taken her into the deep recesses of love. Without her husband and son alive in the physical, her definition of what love is now evolves and changes.

Part of these changes for Donna has been an increase in awareness of not only her husband and son in spirit but also of the presence of others who have passed over. While listening to others talk about their losses at a grief support group she attends, she started to see images of their departed loved ones standing close by. After one meeting, she felt compelled to speak to one of the women who had shared her sadness with the group. Donna hesitantly told the woman of the impressions that she had of the woman's daughter who was now in spirit, whom she had watched smile and gently touch the woman's hand while she spoke of missing her. The woman smiled, tears coming to her eyes. She thanked Donna, explaining that the image of her daughter that Donna had seen described her well.

People who have had many losses and transitions, and have been faced with the unfathomable, often live in the heart of wisdom. They are ignited from within. They face the world, but it cannot claim them. They live with the breath of the eternal alive within them. Often our true gifts emerge as a result of trauma and misfortune.

Maya

Pain and loss often increase intuitive and psychic ability. But it is not necessary to have pain in order to discover our innate gifts and give to others. Maya grew up in South Africa; her father was a geologist, and she has always had a love for stones, crystals, and the natural world. She makes her living as a medical transcriptionist. Her job involves listening to the recordings of medical professionals discussing medical conditions or patient symptoms, and then transcribing what is said. Her job affords her the opportunity to work from her home in rural Virginia.

Due to the many hours she spends on the computer, Maya started to develop carpal tunnel syndrome in both of her arms and hands. Maya told me that she is also aware that while she listens to the recordings describing disease, illness, and pain, she absorbs the energy of what is being said. This at times has left her tired, weary, and sad; as she thinks of the people who may be suffering from these illnesses, her heart is heavy. She feels that this may be another reason why she is developing carpal tunnel; she is tense and she is trying to block the effect that the recordings are having on her.

Maya told me that recently she had the idea that instead of receiving the energy of the doctor's transcript, she could send healing energy through her hands to the documents that she sends back to the doctors. Being the physical intuitive that she is, she is aware of the effect that listening to tapes of illness and disease daily can have on her body, so she has come up with a way to give healing energy instead of receiving harmful energy.

Maya is hopeful that what she is doing is in some way of benefit to others, and she is aware how much better she feels since she has begun to give in this way.

It is important to try not to judge by human terms the importance of our spiritual mission, as we can never truly know the effects our actions will have on others. There is for each one of us a soul plan that has been set in motion from the beginning of time. We are all here to express, create, and evolve into our highest good. We do not have to anxiously try to figure out the best avenue for the expression of our psychic, intuitive gifts. Our soul and our guides will lead us into the experiences and opportunities that speak to our unique abilities and talents.

Spirit reveals our path to us one day at a time; however, we are seldom comfortable with this approach. We would much rather have the overall plans for our life set before us for our careful inspection. Yet this method would appeal too much to our ego, which would then seek to control and direct the flow of events. Rather, when we are open to daily guidance, we soon find that life can be a day-by-day adventure. Our intuition is the bridge connecting us to the inner wise adviser who will show us the way.

18

INTUITIVE
MESSAGES

~~~~~~

Very often the events of our lives are orchestrated in such a way that it is difficult to miss the lesson. At other times, we are unable, as hard as we try, to understand why a situation has come our way. What we experience as fate, luck, or societal limitations are often circumstances that have been set in motion by a combination of factors, including our thoughts and beliefs, our creative ability, our soul purpose, and our karma. By paying attention to the small coincidences of our daily lives and by noticing the many messages sent to us to help us succeed, we can become conscious of what our soul has come here to learn, and we can contribute to our own learning. The choices and decisions we make each day impact how our future unfolds. When we learn to work in unison with the higher energies, we experience less confusion and more harmony.

Our intuitive ability is the tool we can use to access subtle yet powerful directive forces. Our intuition helps us keep ourselves in touch with our inner wisdom. Our intuition can be our most trusted guide in the journey to self-realization. When we spend time listening within, we become more connected to our center, which is the source of love and true power. Understanding our intuitive type or combination of types can help us to connect the outer experience with its inner significance.

We are normally operating in a kind of amnesia. We are disjointed and segmented, seldom able to discern the consequences of our choices. The importance of what happens to us each day can escape our notice and attention, but our intuition can connect the dots. Our inner voice will be honest with us. The conscious mind can babble and chatter unceasingly, but when we allow the quiet voice of our intuition to speak, it will speak the truth. We are discovering the language of Spirit, which comes to us to open our minds, our hearts, and our sense of joy. Guidance usually comes with warmth and humor.

Intuition can show up in our lives in various and surprising ways. We normally work with our intuition from the inside out. We have an inner sense, a feeling, a vision, an unshakable knowing. Sometimes, though, Spirit works very hard to bring our lessons to us in the physical world. As much as we pray and meditate to be guided and given direction, we are often surprised when we get a response. God speaks to us through what we may consider the unremarkable events of our daily lives, and it is not always easy to discern and understand these subtle messages. We expect God to be a linear thinker and to present to us clear guiding markers. Unfortunately, Spirit seldom speaks to us in clear and concise dialogue.

Beatrice

When I met her, Beatrice was the vice-president of a large mortgage company. She had worked hard to get to this position. The hours were long, the work and travel demanding. A few years ago, she began to suffer from diabetes and chronic fatigue syndrome, but despite the aches and pains, she continued to work the long hours her job required.

Several months before I met her, Beatrice changed offices. Her new office had a large window that offered her a view of trees, shrubbery, and flowers. At first she was indifferent to the view. She was too focused in her work to look out the window. But one day as she was working on her computer, she heard the sound of a bird. When she finally looked up, she was confronted with a large raven sitting on a limb directly outside her window. The raven seemed to be watching her. Beatrice was not, however, convinced that the bird could actually see inside the thick window glass.

Then one day, purely out of curiosity, she went outside and looked in. The view was clear! The raven could stare right at her. Day after day, an unspoken exchange between Beatrice and the raven seemed to go on. She would watch the raven and wonder to herself why it had chosen that branch. In reply, the raven would fluff its wings and continue its office vigil. It seemed as if the bird would take flight only when colleagues and clients came inside her office.

Beatrice was puzzled, more puzzled than before. Why doesn't this large, ugly bird just fly away? she asked herself. Why doesn't it go bother someone else? Why wouldn't it leave her alone? By this time, she was both irritated and intrigued by the bird.

She needed an answer. One day during her lunch hour, she went to a bookstore and found several books about animal spirits. Was there a reason for the raven's behavior? Was there a purpose behind its attentiveness to her? What message did this bird have for her? Was she having a crazy thought? How could a bird care for her?

Soon she began to dream about the raven. Next, she started to talk to it. She was sure her friends and family would think she was crazy if she told them of her connection with this bird, but she became more convinced that this bird's presence in her life was no accident. She began to look forward to its visits. The assurance that it would be there, waiting for her, gave her an odd comfort.

The physical intuitive's path was making its presence known in her life. This was more than a new office, a grove of trees, and a strange bird outside her window. Beatrice felt it was a sign, a message for her. She felt less alone. Wondering about her life and her choices, she began to study spiritual topics. She realized that she was just going through the motions in the way she was currently living her life. She longed for a life of meaning and purpose.

One day, Beatrice received a phone call from a friend who was organizing a group of people to go to Louisiana to help the victims of Hurricane Katrina. The friend asked Beatrice if she would be interested in going and helping. Beatrice did not hesitate. She canceled appointments and made arrangements to go. In Louisiana, she spent several weeks helping to clear trash and fallen trees and finding housing for displaced people. Soon she met a recently retired man named Stan, who was devoting his time and talents to helping others. He was a member of the recovery team she was assigned to. They quickly hit it off, finding that they had many common interests. They laughed and worked together. Despite the hard labor, Beatrice had never felt so alive.

She went back home, exhausted but renewed, and continued to communicate with her new friend. Within a few months, she knew what she had to do. She decided to take the talents and knowledge she had acquired in business and pursue a new career. She began a job search and eventually found work at a nonprofit devoted to assisting people displaced by natural disasters. As her career changed, her health improved. Her new job gave her more time to pursue a relationship with Stan, and her love life, long dormant, got a new start. If she had not lived this path herself, she told me, she would hardly be able to believe that her life could have undergone such a transformation. That it seemed to be initiated by a raven was mystifying.

Our guides are just that: our guides. We like to believe they will answer our questions and respond to our needs. And they will do that, but it will always be just a small aspect of their work with us. They want us to be as they are—wise, loving, and fully connected to God.

There is a spiritual agenda. We are foolish to think that the divine shares our self-centered point of view. Our guides and angels are more concerned with our soul's evolution, with eternity. Working with enlightened psychic energy will ultimately lead us into deepening mystery and inner adventure.

The paradox is that we normally go into intuitive growth to get help with our everyday concerns. But accessing information is just the tip of the iceberg. Whatever it is that brings us to intuitive growth is usually just the bread crumbs leading us to a world that we could not have imagined. We will in time be lead into a vastness that will alter our viewpoint of who we are and what reality is. This is the true quest of the spiritual life. It leads us into parts of ourselves that we never knew existed—untapped power, psychic connections with others, unlimited inner resources, and boundless creative possibilities that we believed might belong to others but never to us.

Our world begins to reform itself. We begin to experience a sense of synchronicity and guidance. The feelings of being separate and alone begin to dissipate. The sense of being in this world as a solitary stranger is replaced by the touch of love from a generous universe. Harmony and integration with the spiritual world create a unity in our mind, body, and soul. This leads to an increase in abundance, health, and overall well-being. The gift that Spirit brings to us is the ability to reclaim our heritage as enlightened beings. Along the way, we let go of much of what and who we formerly believed ourselves to be.

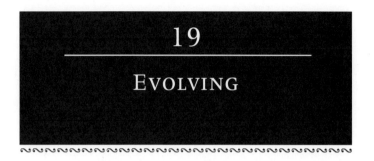

19

EVOLVING

Our evolution into conscious contact with Spirit depends upon our ability to become fluid and changeable. Psychic energy is engaging; it responds to us, it is mutable, it is personal. It interacts with our energy field, and we learn that we are energy meeting energy. We are being guided into unknown territory. It is at this pivotal time, when we are stepping into unfamiliar spirit territory, that we begin to realize that more is required of us. Our personal desires and egotistical concerns bring us more suffering than joy. We learn that we cannot be the recipients of insightful energy for long if we desire only to manipulate it for our personal benefit. When we surrender and let go of our self-centered orientation, we find that we are aided and guided by powerful celestial forces.

Until we are able to quiet the constant influence of the chattering mind, we are not able to fully reap the benefits of our intuition. Our conscious self would like to use intuition as a way to gain access to information that will make our day-to-day lives easier. It wants to know what will happen to us tomorrow and the next day. Most people have concerns in the areas of finances, relationships, and health. Spirit longs to teach us how to manifest and create these material things.

But we must begin in the unseen spiritual world. All that we experience is an extension of this world. Spirit desires love, joy, peace, and serenity for us, just as we do for ourselves. As we search for answers and information, we begin to uncover a deep hidden treasure. We hold the bounty of possibilities within us. We do not have to worry and become stressed out about trying to control the good and make it come our way. God exists within us, always waiting to emerge to activate our highest good.

Surrendering

It is through our free will that we call our inner authority into being. Our personality self does not always realize the value of our inner wisdom. As this shift begins to take place, our intuition seeks to draw from the profound well of inner truth. As we are drawn into a deeper knowing, the difference between what our personality desires and what our soul desires begins to become more evident.

It is through our intuition that we can keep in constant conscious contact with the Source of all that is. When we allow Spirit to lead the way, we find that, unlike our ego, it is gentle and unassuming. Not only that, but Spirit will always be gloriously magnificent; it has no need to go to war against our personality and ego. Spirit smiles at the ego and regards it as a mother would a small child—allowing the will, the desires, and the feelings of righteousness of the child to lead where they will. The soul knows that eventually the child will grow tired, hungry, and lonely in its parade of willful actions.

Intuitive development gives us the tools to lift the veil that normally covers our perceptions. We can become frozen by fear and doubt when we only listen to the voice of the external world. When we focus less on our desired external outcomes and more on our intent and effort, we can be peaceful and centered despite what happens. When we achieve balance between selflessness and Higher Self awareness, we become a conduit for the miraculous. We can experience how the divine molds our individuality to be a perfect vessel for the highest purpose. This can feel like we are working in the dark.

Unlike accessing information, the deep work of soul development can seem to have no immediate purpose. Our first encounters with the psychic world can be profound and even dramatic, but when we enter into the work of spiritual transformation, we work in unison with these powerful forces. This is when we enter into cycles of deep cleansing. Our emotional, mental, spiritual, and physical energy fields undergo profound clearing. Divine energy is light. It is a higher-frequency vibration. Our aura will only be able to absorb this high frequency, where we are free of the heavier, denser material energies. Divine intelligence and love go to work within, clearing and releasing us from whatever would keep us from the realization of our true self. This can be a difficult time for many people.

The Spiritual Night

Although I feel as if I have gone through a few periods of arduous inner growth, there seemed to be no particular occurrence that precipitated a challenging phase for me a few years ago. I was giving an average of twenty-five readings a week, as I had been doing for many years. Many of the people to whom I was giving readings had children and loved ones who had passed over, and they were hopeful that I would be able to connect with these loved ones in spirit. I also had clients who were suffering from various health, financial, and relationship issues. There seemed to be a constant stream of interaction between Spirit and my searching clients, and I had all kinds of help from the spiritual realm. There were grandparents, parents, friends, guides, and angels all present and willing to send messages of hope and support to the people they cared for.

Yet by the end of each day, I would be exhausted. I would prepare for the next day too tired to do much else. I asked my own guides and spiritual helpers if there were a way that I could do readings or schedule my week so as not to be so depleted. I thought that perhaps there would be a way to regulate my energy so that I would not be quite so drained at the end of the day.

The advice that I received surprised me. I was given the message to treat each client and each hour of reading as if it were the only hour, the only session I had. I was told to be "in the now" with each person. So that is what I attempted to do; I began to open completely for each person. I didn't think about the sessions later in the day, or the fact that there were other things I wanted to do that I feared I would not be able to do due to exhaustion. But even with this approach I was still tired, and nothing much seemed to change.

I thought that Spirit seemed awfully concerned for everyone else. I was giving loving guidance and advice to others for their well-being and happiness. Where were my grandparents, loved ones, and angels? Why didn't someone swoop into my consciousness and send love and warmth to me? Instead, I felt little concern from the spiritual world with which I was in daily contact. I felt like an empty psychic shell—no more than a mouthpiece for Spirit. I would tell people that I was Spirit's spokesmodel, but without all the glamour. This continued for what seemed like many months. Even though my psychic abilities were expanding, I was tired, lonely, and I felt unconnected and uncared for in both the spiritual and physical realms.

Eventually, something in me began to give way. I could sense an opening in my heart, but for some reason I resisted it. It felt like an uncomfortable ache. But I had no power to keep those doors closed, and as I gave readings I could feel myself open and energy emerge that I was not completely familiar with. Slowly I surrendered to this feeling and recognized it as love. It was not the personal love that I had come to know; instead, this was a love that seemed to have potent life force and intelligence. It was a love that was beyond my ego and my ability to control. It was a love that knew no limits, and it revitalized me.

Spiritual Cleansing

Each intuitive type will undergo this cleansing process differently. Emotional intuitives may undergo extreme ups and downs. They may have dreams that trigger intense feelings. Allowing such painful emotions to surface and to move through us is often all we are required to do in order to clear ourselves. Emotional intuitives may also feel overwhelmed by others' emotional demands. They may lose touch with their own needs and fail to nurture themselves. Emotional intuitives will sometimes feel selfish if they pay attention to what will fulfill them. With so many people in the world suffering, it can be difficult for emotional intuitives to understand that putting effort into their own sense of peace, joy, and harmony is not self-centered.

Spiritual intuitives may experience this clearing period as a disconnection. They may feel as if they are out of touch. They may question the strength of their union with the spiritual world. Spiritual intuitives may begin to feel too much like wanderers, as if they are drifting meaninglessly through the world. Where once the spiritual realms felt free and unencumbered, spiritual intuitives may now feel as if they are floating in empty, uninspired space. Spiritual intuitives may feel as if they do not have the ability to ground their dreams and purpose. This can create a void, and many spiritual intuitives become spacey and out of touch with the physical and the spiritual.

For mental intuitives, this deep cleansing time may bring them deeper into their own thoughts, and they may feel trapped by their limited belief patterns. An influx of intuitive mental energy will cause confusion and fatigue, with thoughts recycling through the mind like a hamster in a wheel. Mental intuitives may feel as if they are going nowhere, making no progress. They may even question their own intelligence. This may be for them the height of their crisis. They may see expressed in their external lives the manifestations of their thoughts, and this might not make them very happy. As Light makes it way through the mind of the mental intuitive, they will begin to question what they used to view as their foundation, as reality itself.

As the spirituality of physical intuitives deepens, they may feel empty, uninspired, and bored. Their once-strong tie to the earth and her creatures may now manifest in grief and hopelessness, as they conclude that the polluted natural world is doomed to ruin and destruction. They may see the poverty, the sickness, the contamination, and the demise of their natural home. This can be a painful wound that many physical intuitives feel within their own bodies. They are thus prone to get sick during this time. Chronic fatigue, fibromyalgia, environmental sensitivities, and allergies may plague physical intuitives as they are being forced to own their power—physically, mentally, and spiritually. Once the earth harbored all power, beauty, and grace; now they must see it within themselves. They are being drawn into their own soul.

Spiritual Help

All types of intuitives may experience in various ways the crisis that each type undergoes. The time of deepening our spiritual awareness may even shift our predominant intuitive type. It is common to repeat a painful pattern that has surfaced throughout many lifetimes. There will be an increased intensity in our lives. We may feel as if everything we try meets with obstructions and difficulties. Illusions surface, and we may feel that we have been misled and duped by our own spirituality. Previous experiences of divine connection suddenly seem distant. We wonder what got us off the path. Why have we been deserted by our guides and angels?

It is at this time that we need to maintain our awareness that we are in a spiritual process. Our guides will draw closer and help us feel more comfortable and safe. Our intuitive awareness can prove to be invaluable during these trying times. Our Higher Self and our guides take advantage of our vulnerability and energetic shifting. They are able to draw closer and have more influence on us. When we call out for help, our guides are delighted that we have recognized our need for intervention.

Under normal circumstances, our ego is hard to penetrate. We may enjoy spiritual and intuitive pursuits. We may read books and listen to tapes. But when we begin true inner growth, our foundation shifts and we start to break open. We are led to deliberate surrender in many ways. We may have confusing dreams in which buried feelings of pain or fear surface. We could find ourselves in a relationship that brings up a painful pattern of unworthiness and low self-esteem. We may have a physical crisis that draws us to question God's love and grace.

Our crisis could affect us emotionally, physically, mentally, and spiritually. But our angels and guides are patiently waiting close by. They are waiting for us to open to ask for God's love and guidance. And when we yield, the divine enters. We are then able to fully claim our true spiritual nature. This is also when our intuitive potential can begin to be reached. We can open to higher levels of awareness and knowing. We can integrate higher levels of unconditional love. We can be better guided from within. The still, small voice of inner knowing will be stronger, and there will be less static.

Our soulful Higher Self directs our path from within. It has a plan, a path, and a purpose. There is no power stronger in our lives than that of our soul. We have free will to listen to Spirit or to react to the fears and doubts of the material world. When we make choices that are not in keeping with our soul's purpose, it just delays our progress. We can cause ourselves undue suffering, but eventually our soul will find its true path. It is like a river that will find another path or a wider course. The voice of the soul can be subtle, but it can never be muted. When we open our minds, hearts, and spirit, we come closer to understanding the Divine Spirit and God within us. The ultimate goal of psychic, spiritual, and mystical paths is to draw us closer to the divine, the truth of all that is.

20 .

PSYCHIC TO MYSTIC

〜〜〜〜〜〜〜〜〜〜〜〜〜〜〜〜〜〜〜〜〜〜〜〜〜〜〜

Each time I begin a reading for someone, there is a moment of stepping into vacant space. Sometimes it feels as if I am dangling—waiting, active but receptive, hoping for someone or something to show up and speak to me. I have come to expect the unexpected.

When Loni came in for a session, she looked apprehensive and uneasy. She told me she had come to see me on the advice of a friend. She had never been to a "psychic" before, and she was unsure what to expect. I started the reading for Loni, and immediately a woman came through telling me that she was Loni's mother. I was unsure if I was reading this correctly because she had on what looked like a Groucho Marx-type nose and mustache. I didn't say anything to Loni. I thought to myself that she might run out of the room if the first thing I told her is that there is a woman present in spirit who says that she is her mother, but who is wearing what appears to be a fake plastic nose.

As is the case with readings, I could not control what I received. I tried to bypass this image, but felt blocked by it. Loni's mother was laughing and wouldn't go away. I told Loni, "There is a woman coming through who I feel is your mother. She has short grey hair; she is thin and about average height." Loni confirmed that her mother was in spirit, and that this described her physically. I then said, "And she appears to be wearing a fake plastic nose and mustache. Also, there are two other women who just came in and they are all similarly dressed." Loni burst into laughter then began to rifle through her purse. She pulled out a photograph of her mother and her mother's two sisters; they all had on masks and party dresses. In the photo, they were sitting around a table pretending to smoke big cigars.

Developing intuitive and psychic abilities can also at times feel like a leap into the unknown. It may be hard to believe that we have within us the ability to access information or connect to and communicate with the nonphysical. It is also a journey that ignites within us a passion for discovery and revelation.

Psychic Progression

Correctly interpreting intuitive sensations tends to be the biggest hurdle that most people initially encounter. Interpreting psychic energy can be tricky, especially when we are attempting to access guidance for ourselves. We want the events of our lives to unfold in the way that we desire. We want to be financially successful. We want to meet our soul mate. But what we intuitively receive may not seem to speak to our concerns. The images, feelings, thoughts, or impressions that surface may not make sense to us. We may wonder if we are interpreting our psychic impressions to coincide with what we most want or with what we most fear. We may become confused. We may wonder if we are only fooling ourselves.

When we begin working with intuitive energy, we expect and desire information. When we enter the deeper waters of psychic development, we begin to live with the inner knowledge that all is well. We come to the realization that there is an inner guide, a plan that we can trust, and we have less need to know the details. Even when we are confronted by illness, loss, or pain, we find a way opening. We are no longer bound by conditions, and we are not overly concerned and fearful of the future. We can feel the comfort that surrounds us and cares for us. When we release ourselves into the mystical realm, we enter into a higher knowing. This is not merely the knowing of events or future conditions, however; it is an understanding and transcendence into the creative now.

Sequana has had many readings from many different psychics. She came to me wanting to know if she will find her soul mate. She wanted to know what he will look like and when he will appear in her life. It was easy to read in Sequana's energy the men who will be entering her life. She was impressed by my accuracy, but she was less than thrilled by the quality of men I predicted would come her way. She draws to her the same kind of man over and over—men who look wonderful but who lack maturity and a willingness to commit. These are not the kind of men she wants, but these are the men who keep coming to her.

Like many of us, Sequana understands neither her power nor her free will. Without knowing it, we usually create our present from our past. Because we do this without realizing it, we normally limit what comes into our lives. When we enter the mystical realm and release our need to control our lives from an ego level, our intuition will quietly nudge and prod us to move beyond our self-imposed limitations.

Spirit always creates from unconditional love, wisdom, and joy. We have been given the freedom to create and to choose what we draw to us. We can choose to create from the human mind like Sequana is doing, or we can release the outcome to the divine within us. When we choose the divine, we must be willing to surrender control. We have to willingly give up our need to direct what will come our way, and when and how.

Divine Spirit always does a better job than we do. We do not always know where our bliss lies. When we allow intuitive or spiritual development to unfold within us, we find that we are more able to trust and act on the guidance that we are given, even when it may seem to be illogical or impractical.

The world continues to clamor with issues and problems, but we are better able to hear the subtle inner voice that quietly guides us through the chaos. We also have more clarity as to what our intuition is telling us. We can distinguish between what is legitimate intuitive insight and what is simply our hopeful imaginings.

As Sequana's intuition strengthens, she will be better able to know that when she lets go, there is a power, a presence, a force that will catch her. We do not release our cares to Spirit because we fear there may be only empty space there, or because we believe that Spirit cannot possibly care for our individual needs and concerns. Psychic energy focused in the mystical realm assures us this is not so. We can feel the love and the connections surrounding us and within us. This may feel like the brush of an angel's wing, our name being gently called, or an inner knowing that cannot be shaken by outer appearances.

When we are attuned to mystical insight, we do not *hope*; we *know*. We have a tangible awareness. It is a comfort that cannot be described. No one can fully comprehend what will unfold in the outer world, but we can live each hour, each day knowing that we are precious and that we are being guided into bliss. As we come into the mystical and divine realms, our sense of security comes from within us. Spirit works in paradox. The mystical realm can be obscure and comforting at the same time. It calls us to be transformed, to expect the unexpected. Simply knowing outcomes becomes less important. We yearn instead for constant conscious connection with a Higher Power. Our intuitive type becomes our spiritual path.

We will not only be able to receive guidance to help us with our everyday concerns, but we are also led into the deeper mystery of life. Intuition first guides us into self-knowledge, and then it opens the door into the Higher Self. When we live from the divine within, we participate in the world but are not bound by it.

Our pure Self, our soul, is creative and transcendent. Without the ability to experience the beauty of the soul, we can become all form and no substance. Our lives may seem like an endless stream of inconsequential and meaningless experiences. It is like the difference between a live vibrant rose and a picture of a rose—which, however beautifully it is painted, lacks the essence and fragrance of a living flower. When we engage our psychic energy with the desire to know truth, deep transformative forces shape and mold us. We live in the grandeur of soul. The gateway to wisdom and unconditional love is always open, always calling to us to enter.

The reward of developing psychic ability is not just in knowing the outcomes of events or in predicting the future. The lasting gift of psychic ability is harnessing the inner power of our spirit by establishing within ourselves the ability to communicate and create from the depths of truth, wisdom, and the eternal.

Integrating Types

Intuitive types are like archetypal blueprints that, when followed, can lead to greater awareness of our lives and our soul path. Our type is like a river leading us to the vast sea. Our soul feeds us from the true substance, asking us to see our reflection in that eternal sea. Our intuitive awareness enables us to set sail and explore the immensity of existence. Our intuitive type is not restrictive. It is the vessel on which we sail—on which we sail and learn how to live in the unseen.

The goal of developing our intuitive and psychic ability by understanding our type is both to fully and internally integrate the four types and then to transcend them. As we grow in psychic and spiritual awareness, we come to a turning point that we all will eventually encounter. We first work with psychic, spiritual energy at the level we find comfortable. We come to this energy through the mental, physical, emotional, or spiritual approach. During this process, our growth may be rapid. We may feel confidant and embrace the process. Then we are given a choice. We can grow beyond ourselves, beyond our level of comfort and control. Or we can stall and withdraw.

It can be difficult to step out of what we consider the norm, and we find ourselves fearful at times. It might be that we worry that inner transformation will result in loss or change in our external life. We may fear rejection by family and friends or loss of income and social acceptance. We may be apprehensive about the unknown and the spacious freedom that lies before us. Yet it is only at this juncture, when our fears are most intense, that we can transcend our limitations and glimpse our true potential.

The journey of psychic awareness ultimately leads us to the conscious realization of our oneness with all of life. Within this oneness there exists all that is. All the past, the present, and the creative possibilities of the future coexist as energy.

When we consciously merge into the center of pure consciousness, we transcend time and space and therefore have access to all that we desire. In order for our normal consciousness to ascend into higher awareness and operate from a broader perspective of life, it is necessary that we know how to receive and embrace these higher vibrations. We will never be able to completely quiet the ego-personality part of ourselves and it is not necessary that we do so. Instead, it is important to focus attention on our more soulful aspects.

With practice we can learn how to activate our mind, body, heart, and spirit to unify and reside in the awareness of all that is. When we attempt to read energy—whether it be clairvoyantly, telepathically, empathetically, or through psychometry—it is important that our efforts are fueled by higher-level psychic currents. When we draw only from the small-ego-personality self, our results will be limited. We will also exhaust our physical body and be more likely to interpret the information we receive based on our personal biases and beliefs. Psychic information should help us to understand our lives from a broader perspective. We should feel a connection and be uplifted by what we receive.

This meditative exercise can be practiced by everyone. It will help to integrate and lift awareness into higher consciousness. Daily practice of this mediation will open new doors of awareness and integration, as it will help our energy to expand beyond our preconceived limitations.

The Experience of Oneness Meditation

- Draw your attention within your body and deeply inhale. Feel your body energized and relaxed by the breath. Feel the breath circulate throughout your body. Exhale and release any tension and stress. Draw your breath from the top of the head and send it down to the soles of the feet. Feel the soles of your feet firmly on the ground. Imagine that you can draw energy from the earth into your feet, and then that you can send that energy throughout the body. Continue to draw energy from the earth. Draw it into the body, and feel the body expand beyond the physical body. Imagine the earth embracing you, energizing you; it has called you here, into physical existence. The sun, the moon, and the stars create a network of energy, from which you can draw your life force. You exist within this beautiful web of creation. Within this sparkling energetic substance there is perfect harmony. Feel your heartbeat. It is the heartbeat of all that is, resounding through and transcending time and space. The earth, her creatures, the skies accept you as their own.

- Feel your heart, breathe into the heart, and exhale through the heart. Feel it open and expand. As you breathe and exhale through the heart, feel it open as you accept whatever feelings emerge. Pay attention to them. Now draw your breath from the life force that surrounds you. It is love. You now breathe from the center of love, and with each breath this love expands.

Love surrounds you. You can send this love outward to whomever or whatever you desire. You can send this love inward, healing any inner pain or guilt. This love has intelligence and purpose. You are nurtured and cared for; you can release yourself to this love. You are one with the love of the universe. Love is the glue of the universe; it resides within you. Love sustains you. Love is you.

- Merge into this love and become love. Experience the interconnectedness of all that is. Your thoughts allow you to know and to experience. Contemplate and rest in the pure knowledge that exists within you. Thought gives meaning to what is. Where is your mind? Breathe into the mind. It is the energy that surrounds you. It is the invigorating stuff of consciousness that exists in all that is. Expand into consciousness and allow all the beliefs and boundaries that separate you from pure knowing to dissolve. Your mind merges with the intelligence of all of life. Consciousness is invisible, palatable; it creates order and unity within the universe. You are connected to the spring of all being, where the past, present, and future reside. You easily become one with wisdom.

- You dissolve into wisdom, into consciousness, yet you are aware and alert while you freely move beyond form. You observe the body, the mind, the heart, but you are not these; you are unencumbered and free. With calm focus you can experience anything and everything. You can go to any distant location. You can visit any reality. You can experience any state of being that you desire and feel any emotion. Then you can move out of that experience and back into freedom. You are one with all that is. You are free.

- Now breathe this freedom and sense of oneness into the body. Feel the oneness as love, as wisdom and unity. Be open and receptive to any messages and further shifts in awareness and knowing that may occur. Surrender to the experience and allow it to continue to unfold.

This meditative exercise will lift the small self-ego perception that we normally operate under into the broader experience of oneness. It will increase the flow of higher vibrational energy into the body, mind, and spirit. This will have the effect of expanding the energy field and charging our inner psychic battery with fuel.

We do not go to heaven; we grow into heaven. The changes that we experience in perception will also expand our aura and energy field. This in turn will invigorate and strengthen our psychic perception. We will energetically open ourselves to a multidimensional awareness. Altered states of consciousness will be more likely to occur, as will the ability to astral travel, channel, and come into contact with nonphysical, intelligent life forms.

Kara

Kara initially called me because she was concerned about her health. She had not felt well for a long time, and she wanted to heal. Yet despite her efforts, her health continued to decline. She had been diagnosed with chronic fatigue syndrome and diabetes. In my initial session with Kara, I was surprised by the inner power that I felt was locked up inside of her, even though she was exhausted all the time and on some days barely able to get out of bed. Kara was unable to access the deep inner reserve of energy that she needed for her health and well-being.

Many years ago Kara had a group of friends who were all interested in psychic and paranormal phenomena; they experimented with their psychic abilities and Kara discovered she had unexpected talent. She soon began to have dreams that foretold future events in her life and those of her friends. One night she had a dream in which a friend of hers drowned in a deep whirlpool. Kara woke up anxious and perplexed by the dream. Eventually she reasoned it away as not a literal future happening, but as a symbolic representation of what her friend was going through emotionally.

Then the unexpected happened. She received a call one morning from a friend. Their mutual friend, the woman that Kara had dreamed of, had drowned. She had been rafting down a swollen river; she got caught in the strong current and fell off the raft and drowned. Kara shut down. She felt that she had been given a message in her dream that she ignored. She was angry at herself and at God. This was the beginning of Kara's decline in health.

Over time Kara began to understand the importance of forgiving herself and opening up to life again. She was hesitant, but eventually, little by little, she began to heal. Her health began to improve, and she started to feel physically stronger than she had in a long time. Along with this healing, her psychic ability once again emerged. She started to dream again and to receive psychic impressions while awake. She was tempted to try and shut them down, but she knew too well the repercussions that could result if she were to do so. Instead, Kara began to meditate, to go within herself and ask for clear guidance. Understanding her spiritual and psychic ability became as much a priority for her as improving her physical health.

Since my first session with Kara a few years ago, her life has changed quite a bit. Not only is she physically much healthier, but her psychic life has also evolved. She recently called me to share an experience she had while listening to a woman lecture at a convention on spiritual matters. Kara told me that while she sat listening to this speaker, she felt an incredible rush of love well up within her heart. She felt love flow through her in waves, reaching out to anyone in the room or beyond who was in need of it. The love was stimulating and revitalizing; she felt her whole body become warmer as the love flowed through her.

Next, Kara felt a tingling in her head and, with a burst of energy, she felt the top of her head open. She told me that it felt like the proverbial lotus blooming and spreading its petals outward. She felt wisdom and a deep knowing rise within her. The energy seemed to cascade down her spine, filling her with even more warmth and feelings of pleasure. She stayed in this state for a time, allowing the experience to unfold.

Eventually she looked around the room, assuming that perhaps others were also experiencing some level of spiritual awakening. But this was not the case. Instead, the others in the room seemed to be listening and focusing on the speaker. No one else looked flushed and altered.

With Kara's acceptance of her spiritual and psychic energy have come transcendental experiences. She feels blessed by these occurrences and deeply grateful for the wisdom, joy, and love that accompany them.

Changes in the Energy Field

When we enter into the mystical realm, we experience the boundlessness of existence. Whereas we once used psychic energy in the world, when we enter the mystical realm we draw our attention within. Our ability to discern the subtle realities is heightened. We enter a world beyond outward appearances. We can use our psychic energy to contemplate heavenly realms. This oneness is always present. Through our intuition we can be in constant communion with source. As we turn our consciousness to a spiritual orientation, the outer material world loses its hold on us.

As powerful as we perceive our present conditions to be, they can never limit and control our spirit. We no longer need to believe that something is real only if it can be measured and quantified in physical terms. Our energy field changes as we listen to our intuition and trust it and act on it. Whatever we give energy to grows. Just as our physical bodies become fit when we exercise, so too our psychic sensitivity will grow and refine itself when we exercise it. Our energy field becomes stronger. When we live in the world with the belief that everything is random and of no consequence, we may experience an increase in anxiety and fear. We may shrink and draw into ourselves in a protective stance, cutting ourselves off and suffering emotionally, spiritually, mentally, and physically.

When we engage our spirit, however, and trust that we are intimately connected to all of life—even without the kind of tangible physical evidence that we sometimes feel we need—we are fed from the root, the well, the center. We create within our aura a crystalline axis of light. We are no longer simply cell, tissue, organ, blood, and bone. The speck of soul that dwells within expands and fills us, and we become an instrument for the working out of a higher intelligence and love. This is the mysterious process that leads us to the experience of mystical states. During this progression of inner soul refinement, we break down and dissolve the beliefs, judgments, and negativity that has kept us from full enlightenment and awareness. We will be transformed and our true nature revealed. Psychic energy gives us the tools for conscious union.

As we are more able to perceive the sublime, we will live more fully in the consciousness of divine realization and we will find that all things speak to us. They wish for us to commune with them. The angels and archangels and our loved ones in spirit live right beside us. They are not far away. There is not time and space. There is only here, only now. They constantly whisper "eternity" in our ears, waking us to this divine Truth.

21

THE MYSTICAL GIFTS

A s our intuitive type evolves, we move through the experiences of all four types and at the same time go beyond them. We have within us all that is. Therefore it would make sense that we can encounter the spiritual richness and potential of each type, for the path of every type eventually leads us to the same place: the experience of our true self. Our growth is along a spiral wave of energy that leads us into awareness, love, and light. Each intuitive type holds the key to the experience of mystical states.

Admission into mystical states is in large part a mysterious process. It is not by being "good" and "moral" that we will know God. It is by grace that the veil is lifted. It is through inner communion with the divine that our soul slips into the mystical. With trust and courage we can release ourselves into the celestial currents. Although our human self may feel fear and apprehension as we let go of our hold on the known, we soon become accustomed to the feel of spiritual freedom. It is a balm to our weary, control-driven "normal" life. Reality becomes pliable, re-creating itself in the reflection of our consciousness. As we surrender and allow our soul to unite with its Creator, magnetic forces draw us into the divine radiance. We will have moments when time stands still and we experience oneness. The mystical is not easily spoken of, not easily put into words, but when we have entered the kingdom, we will know, our heart will know, our soul and even our body will know.

The Emotional Intuitive

The emotional intuitive is on the path of heart. As emotional intuitives enter the mystical realm, they move into unconditional love and compassion. The human gives way to the divine. This is the journey from emotional awareness to heart-centeredness. When emotional intuitives are fully evolved, their ability to love transcends the confines of conditional and co-dependent love. Their love becomes the love of the divine moving through them into the suffering world.

This love is not based on the individual, the personality, or the ego. Emotional intuitives can sit in a room and send healing rays of divine love to those a few miles or thousands of miles away. Compassion and unconditional love are not bound by time or space. Emotional intuitives know love as a powerful agent for healing. They can heal and bless others through compassion and forgiveness. They are able to transform feelings like fear, guilt, and anger into higher states of awareness and compassion. The floodgates of love open for the emotional intuitive, and they bathe themselves and others in the purity of love's cleansing currents. Desiring to live in the center, united and whole, they perceive love in all things. The mystical heart seeks union with its beloved.

> *When I glow*
> *When I glow*
> *You must shine,*
> *When I flow*
> *You must be laved.*
> *When you sigh*
> *You draw my heart, God's heart, into yourself.*
> *When you weep for me*
> *I take you in my arms.*
> *But when you love*
> *We two shall be as one.*
> *When we are one at last, then none*
> *Can ever make us part again,*
> *Unending, wishless rapture*
> *Shall dwell between us twain.*[16]
> —Mechthild of Magdeburg (1210–1285)

The Mental Intuitive

For mental intuitives, the journey is into the mind of God, into the realm of the creative and the all-knowing. As the mental intuitive enters the mystical realm, the human mind gives way to enlightened awareness. The mind of the mental intuitive glows with the rays of pure, omnipotent enlightened intelligence; they fuse with wisdom. When we know God intimately, we know God's thoughts. This may bring the gift of prophecy, the foreknowledge of events. Mental intuitives bring the ideas of the divine to humanity. They can reveal to each soul its destiny. They can discern Truth. As the eighth-century Sufi mystic Rabia of Basra wrote:

> My understanding used to be like a stream
> That easily described all along the bank as its ken moved
> through the world.
> When I entered God, my vision became like His,
> It flooded out over existence,
> I knew no limits.
> The future I can now see with as much certainty
> as the past.
> If I stretched my arm its full length
> I could caress any creature in this universe;
> And Rabia does not
> exaggerate. [17]

The Physical Intuitive

The physical intuitive walks this earth with the divine. When physical intuitives enter the mystical realm, they perceive all things as holy. They move from the concrete to the transcendent, and then with divine grace these two seemingly opposing states become one. In their fully evolved state, they are capable of transmitting healing to those who are ill or in pain. Their touch can send out waves of Divine Light that uplift those in need. They are divine magicians who are not bound by the physical. They move through matter and density, dissolving them at will as the physical and the spiritual become one. Purity flows through them in streams of light, giving us the vision of earthly perfection. Their gift is the creation of heaven on earth. They call us to this knowing. Here is the medieval visionary and poet Hildegard von Bingen's description:

> *O flower, you did not spring from the dew*
> *nor from drops of rain,*
> *nor did the air sweep over you,*
> *but the divine radiance*
> *brought you forth on a most noble branch.*
> *O branch, God had foreseen your flowering*
> *on the first day*
> *of creation.*[18]

The Spiritual Intuitive

The spiritual intuitive lives in the physical world, with the essence of spirit always close. Their mystical calling is that of full immersion into the unseen and, paradoxically, full union with heaven and earth. They can reach ecstatic states of rapture and communion with the saints, the angels, and the divine. With their touch, their look, and their prayers, spiritual intuitives can draw others into these elusive, blissful states. They are able to transcend our worldly fears and concerns. They conceive of other realities, of another existence not bound by what we perceive as the "real world."

With the mystical spiritual intuitive, we live in timeless eternity. In their eyes we can see our souls, freely dancing in ecstasy with the divine. They give us the gift of spiritual freedom; they see and live beyond the veil. Saint Teresa of Avila had this gift, which she described as follows:

There is a divine world of light
with many suns in
the sky.
I slept with my Lord
one night,
now all that is luminous
I know we
conceived. [19]

The human energy field extends into the divine. We have within ourselves the passageway to the heavens. Our energy can be seen as a spiraling cocoon of vibration. We have angelic wings that lift us into the celestial. We are ethereal souls, circling in the luminance of all light, anchored and nurtured by the spirit of our beautiful Earth. This is our loving home— nestled in fields of flowers, whispered to by gentle waves, and soothed in the breeze. Our hearts are the clear channels of healing and compassion. We nurture and receive; we are the ebb and flow of the divine.

SOURCES

1. Bletzer, June. *The Encyclopedic Psychic Dictionary*. Lithia Springs, GA: New Leaf, 1986, 323.

2. *The Oxford Essential Quotations Dictionary*. New York: Berkley, 1998, 222.

3. Teresa, Mother, and Thomas Moore. *No Greater Love*. Novato, CA: New World Library, 2001, 30.

4. Einstein, Albert. *The World As I See It*. Filiquarian Publishing, 2006, 15. [Title originally published in 1934.]

5. Ibid., 37.

6. *The Oxford Essential Quotations Dictionary*. New York: Berkley, 1998, 64.

7. Cummings, Stephen, and Dana Ullman. *Everybody's Guide to Homeopathic Medicines*. New York: Tarcher/Penguin, 2004, 19.

8. Cayce, Edgar, and Jeffrey Furst, ed. *Edgar Cayce's Story of Jesus*. New York: Berkley, 1976, 131.

9. Ibid., 131.

10. Cayce, Edgar, and Harmon H. Bro. *Edgar Cayce on Dreams*. Avenel, NJ: Wings Books, 1969, 39.

11. Osho. *The Buddha Said* . . . New York: Sterling Publishing, 2007, 187.

12. Ibid., 444.

13. Bletzer, June G. *The Encyclopedic Psychic Dictionary*. Lithia Springs, GA: New Leaf, 1986, 354.

14. Chopra, Deepak. *Creating Affluence*. San Rafael, CA: New World Library, 1998, 85.

15. Rumi, and Coleman Barks, trans. *The Essential Rumi*. New York: HarperCollins, 1995, 243.

16. Reinhold, H. A., ed. *The Soul Afire: Revelations of the Mystics*. Garden City, NY: Image Books, 1973, 292.

17. Various, and Daniel Ladinsky, trans. *Love Poems from God: Twelve Sacred Voices from the East and West*. New York: Penguin, 2002, 25.

18. Hildegard von Bingen, and Jane Bobko, ed. *Vision: The Life and Music of Hildegard von Bingen*. New York: Studio, 1995, 77.

19. Various, and Daniel Ladinsky, trans. *Love Poems from God: Twelve Sacred Voices from the East and West*. New York: Penguin, 2002, 288.

Psychic Development for Beginners

An Easy Guide to Releasing and Developing Your Psychic Abilities

WILLIAM HEWITT

Psychic Development for Beginners provides detailed instruction on developing your sixth sense, or psychic ability. Improve your sense of worth, your sense of responsibility, and therefore your ability to make a difference in the world. Innovative exercises like "The Skyscraper" allow beginning students of psychic development to quickly realize personal and material gain through their own natural talent.

Benefits range from the practical to the spiritual. Find a parking space anywhere, handle a difficult salesperson, choose a compatible partner, and even access different time periods! Practice psychic healing on pets or humans—and be pleasantly surprised by your results. Use psychic commands to prevent dozing while driving. Preview out-of-body travel, cosmic consciousness, and other alternative realities. Instruction in *Psychic Development for Beginners* is supported by personal anecdotes, forty-four psychic development exercises, and twenty-eight related psychic case studies designed to help students gain a comprehensive understanding of the psychic realm.

978-1-5671-8360-3
216 pages

$11.95

To order, call 1-877-NEW-WRLD
Prices subject to change without notice

Practical Guide to
Psychic Powers
DENNING & PHILLIPS

Because you are missing out on so much without them! Who has not dreamed of possessing powers to move objects without physically touching them, to see at a distance or into the future, to know another's thoughts, to read the past of an object or person, or to find water or mineral wealth by dowsing?

This book is a complete course—teaching you step-by-step how to develop the powers that actually have been yours since birth. Psychic powers are a natural part of your mind. By expanding your mind in this way, you will gain health and vitality, emotional strength, greater success in your daily pursuits, and a new understanding of your inner self.

You'll learn to play with these new skills, working with groups of friends to accomplish things you never would have believed possible. The text shows you how to make the equipment, do the exercises— many of them at any time, anywhere—and how to use your abilities to change your life and the lives of those close to you.

978-0-8754-2191-9
216 pages

$11.95

Soul Mates

Understanding Relationships Across Time

RICHARD WEBSTER

The eternal question: how do you find your soul mate—that special, magical person with whom you have spent many previous incarnations? Popular metaphysical author Richard Webster explores every aspect of the soul mate phenomenon in this book.

The incredible soul mate connection allows you and your partner to progress even further with your souls' growth and development with each incarnation. *Soul Mates* begins by explaining reincarnation, karma, and the soul, and prepares you to attract your soul mate to you. After reading examples of soul mates from the author's own practice, and famous soul mates from history, you will learn how to recall your past lives. In addition, you will gain valuable tips on how to strengthen your relationship so that it grows stronger and better as time goes by.

978-1-5671-8789-2
240 pages

$13.95

To order, call 1-877-NEW-WRLD